JESUS. EVERYDAY GOOD NEWS

Healing Thoughts for Broken People

Sharon Pergerson
Chernae Saka
Oliver Nelson

TABLE OF CONTENTS

Section 1

Section 2

Section 3

DEDICATION AND ACKNOWLEGEMENTS

First and foremost, we dedicate this book to Jesus, Christ, the Lover of our souls. From birth, He has maneuvered our lives towards finding and knowing Him and towards a friendship and teamwork that spans over a decade. At a critical juncture in each of our lives, God used Pastor William Pergerson, II to rewire our minds by focusing our attention on the power and beauty of the character of Jesus Christ. With each revelation of Jesus, we all found that He is indeed altogether lovely and matchlessly charming. As a result of our focus on Him and His righteousness, our love for Him and for those He loves continues to increase. In all our experiences, good and painful, individual and collective, Jesus has been and is our all-sufficiency. We can't help but share our thoughts about Him with as many as will listen and read.

In addition, it has been a joy to work on this first book together. We have each been blessed by each other's *"thoughts"*. The Bible tells us that King David, during a difficult time in His life, encouraged himself in the Lord his God (1 Sam. 30:6). In this book, we are doing the same, encouraging ourselves in the Lord our God and bringing you on the journey with us.

We thank our families and team who encouraged us to keep writing, Dr. Walton Whaley who helped us with editing, the many young people in our lives who keep us on our knees, and who helped us unload any unnecessary fluff from our writing, and the many others who pray for us and our mission. We are so honored to have you all in our lives, and as a part of this book. May each of you, along with all our readers be as blessed as we have been as you read the *"thoughts"* God shared with us to share with you.

INTRODUCTION

Dear Readers,

One moment, life can feel like a calm stroll along the beach shore with the peaceful ocean lapping at our feet and our minds at rest without a care in the world. In the next minute, life can feel like a raging ocean chasing us down with relentless fury eager to destroy us, and leaving us feeling like, no matter how hard we try, we cannot outrun or outswim it. In such moments, we feel our human vulnerability, and we recognize our need for something, rather Someone, greater than ourselves—the only Source who can rescue, heal, and empower us to rise, fight, overcome, and thrive once more.

In those darkest moments of life, our hope eventually dwindles down to only God and His Word, regardless of our beliefs. That is all we have to hold on to, to keep us sane, and to lift us up from the bottomless pit of despair and hopelessness. We believe that God's Word is full of the power we need for all our brokenness. Thus, in this book, healing Bible verses are used as the foundation and authority of our *thoughts*.

Our only motive is to focus on Jesus as the everyday good news for broken people. The *thoughts* in this book are from our own experiences as heartbroken children of God who have seen and felt life's moments of joys and devastation, and who have experienced the sweet peacemaking presence of Jesus Christ through it all. Our prayer is that our *thoughts* will encourage you, strengthen your faith in God, and remind you that you are never alone, Jesus is your everyday good news.

Most sincerely,

Sharon Pergerson, Chernae Saka, and Oliver Nelson

SECTION ONE

As broken people we all need everyday good news reminders about what God has already done for us in Jesus Christ.

01

Jesus. Everyday Good News

THE SEARCH FOR REAL LOVE

Sharon Pergerson

The steadfast love of the LORD never ceases; His mercies never come to an end; they are new every morning; great is your faithfulness. (Lamentations 3:22-23, ESV)

Have you ever felt afraid of love? Has love ever made you feel like you were on a rollercoaster ride? One moment, it leaves you feeling you are on top of the world; the next minute, you feel like it has dropped you so low you want to crawl under the world. Regardless, love is a rare commodity that every person in the world longs for. Sadly, though so desired, human love is riddled with so many distortions that one is often left wondering, "*What is real love*?"

In the English language, one word, love, is used to describe all types of love, while in the Greek (the original language the New Testament was written in), four different words are used. Eros describes romantic love between a man and a woman. Philo describes brotherly or friendship love. Storge describes family love, and Agape describes God's selfless love. Agape is an extraordinary love that is used only in the context of God's love. The uniqueness of Agape is that it is unconditional, changeless, and selfless. God's unconditional love originates from His goodness and not ours. Bible verses such as Romans 5:6-10 and Titus 3:3-6 remind us that while we were sinning, disobedient, weak, and enemies of God, He demonstrated His love (Agape) for us to its depths.

Martin Luther, the reformer, summarized that God doesn't love us because of our worth; we are of worth because He loves us. God is love, and He loves everyone, whether we think we are good or bad, because He alone is always good. His Agape is changeless, unending, everlasting, and never fails. Jeremiah 31:3 reminds us that God loves us with an everlasting love. 1 Corinthians 13:8 reminds us that God's love never fails, and Romans 8:35-39 reminds us that nothing and no one can separate us from the love of God.

Lastly, God's Agape is selfless, self-emptying, and self-giving. It is other-centered and thus will descend for the benefit of others. In Philippians 2:4-8 and Hebrews 2:9, we see that when Jesus descended, he emptied Himself of self, to be made like us so that He could taste the death that was ours as the penalty for our wrongdoing. There is no selfishness in God's agape. Have you noticed how, in 1 Corinthians 13, the word charity is used in most translations? The word charity today expresses humanity's best love towards one another. While charity has done some nice things, we all know our best human love is always tainted with some sort of selfishness. 1 Corinthians 13:4-8 does not describe charity, humanity's best love towards one another; it describes God's agape, the ONLY selfless love.

Thank God His Agape is in complete contradiction to our messed-up human love. While we do get glimpses of God's love in some of our relationships, we have all experienced how human love is conditional. It changes, ends, fails, and is selfish and self-centered. Many people do not realize that the search for human love to satisfy the longings of their hearts is a futile hope. The only real love that satisfies completely and consistently is God's Agape. This great love is what God demonstrates to us in the birth, life, death, and resurrection of Jesus (Romans 5:8-11), and which He freely sheds abroad to every heart (Romans 5:5), including yours and mine. In Jesus Christ, our search for real love comes to a glorious end.

Good News Prayer

Jesus, You know my need. Your Agape doesn't take me on rollercoaster rides like other 'loves' do. Your Agape is the most powerful force in the universe, and I joyfully receive it. It stabilizes me. Now, my mind and heart can rest in Your Agape for me because it is unconditional, changeless, and selfless. As I respond to Your Agape, please cause it to flow through me to others who need to see Your 'real love'. Thank You and amen.

01

Jesus. Everyday Good News

THE SEARCH FOR REAL LOVE

Sharon Pergerson

My Reflections on "the Search for Real Love"

02

Jesus. Everyday Good News

A LESSON FROM THE SKY

Sharon Pergerson

The heavens declare His righteousness, and all people see His glory.
(Psalms 97:6, KJV)

Next time you are outside, or as soon as you can go outside, look up at the clear, blue sky and think about how, no matter where we are in the world, no matter our circumstances, no matter the weather, and no matter how we feel, the sky is always there. If we are in a low valley or on top of the tallest mountain, the same sky is still there, as far as the east is from the west. Regardless of the state of our community, nation, world, or relationships, one of the few things we know for sure is that the sky will be there in the morning, and the sky will be there at night, faithful and steady, every day.

It's as if the sky is a monumental reminder of something grand, something we need and long for every day. What could that be? Maybe it's a deep desire to understand God's true character and how He feels about us. I believe the sky reminds us that God loves and cares for every one of us and that He is with us no matter where we are in the world, no matter our circumstances, no matter the turbulent and difficult times we live in, and no matter how we feel. He is always here for us, faithful and steady, every day. His love and care for us never change. We might be in a low valley of despair or on top of the tallest mountain of prosperity, but the same God is still right there with us.

What about the storms, when the sky turns angry and dark, when the lightning flashes, and the thunder rolls? God is still there. Psalms 18:11 tells us that God makes darkness His secret place, His pavilion. What do I believe that means for you and me? To me, it means that God moves even closer to us during our darkest times. He sets up house with us in our most painful and scariest situations. He comes to suffer with us. He comes to comfort us and wrap us in his loving

A LESSON FROM THE SKY

Sharon Pergerson

arms. He and we are in this life together until one day soon, He breaks through those skies and receives us to Himself.

Good News Prayer

Dear Jesus, every time I look up at the sky, may I be reminded of Your love for me, in good times and bad times. The lessons from Your heavens give me strength to face each day with hope and courage because I know that You are my constant stability amid so much confusion, pain, and insecurity. You, the God of all creation, are with me. You love and care for me personally and always. I thank You and receive You into my heart today and every day. Amen.

02

Jesus. Everyday Good News

A LESSON FROM THE SKY

Sharon Pergerson

My Reflections on "A Lesson from the Sky"

03

Jesus. Everyday Good News

THE SURE WORD OF FAITH

Oliver Nelson, III

So then faith cometh by hearing and hearing by the word of God. (Romans 10:17, KJV)

Biblical faith is a fascinating topic. As I reflect on it, I have found that faith is not feeling. Faith is not an action dictated by my circumstances. I have come to understand that Biblical faith is making the conscious decision to depend solely, exclusively, and entirely upon the Word of God to accomplish what it says. The Word of God always accomplishes what it says because it is alive, full of power, and sharper than any sword with two edges (Hebrews 4:12-17). Additionally, the Word of God always accomplishes what it says because the Word itself is imbued with God's creative power (Isaiah 55:11).

Think about God's Word and how at creation He spoke, and whenever He spoke, that which He spoke (the Sun, Moon, Stars, sky, etc.) immediately came into existence (see Genesis 1, Psalm 33:6-9). Then, in the New Testament, notice Jesus's interaction with the Roman centurion in Matthew 8:5-10. The centurion asked Jesus to heal his servant. Jesus responded by saying that He would come to the centurion's home and do so, but the centurion, who seemed to understand the creative power of God's Word, expressed to Jesus that if He, Jesus, simply spoke the Word only, his servant would be healed.

That story and many others show us that God's Word is not some magical word written down in the Bible with its own power source, The power of the Word comes from Jesus, who is the living Word of God (John 1:1-2, 14). Think about it, the "Word of God is from the "*Word*" of God, Jesus. He is the living Word of God who became human and lived among us. As we read and receive the Word of God into our hearts, we are actually receiving the "Word" of God, Jesus Christ, into our hearts.

03

Jesus. Everyday Good News

THE SURE WORD OF FAITH

Oliver Nelson, III

Today, we live on a planet filled with uncertainty. Every day, we read headline after headline about the senseless loss of life across the globe. The ebbs and flows of our economy can result in our financial stability one day and financial ruin the next. During doctor visits, our stomachs clench with fear from the prospect of a doctor telling us that we have contracted a fatal disease.

While there is little certainty in this life, the one thing that we can be sure of is that God's creative Word never fails because Jesus never fails. No wonder John in Revelation 19:13 described Jesus as wearing a robe dipped in the blood of His own life (given for us) and His name being called, *"the Word of God"*. His Word to us always accomplishes what it says and if we receive Him through His creative Word today, by faith, that Word will work in us both to will and to do what is according to God's good divine purpose for us (Philippians 2:13).

Everyday Good News Prayer:

"Dearest Jesus, the Bible contains Your Word from You to me and is my only certainty. Every promise in it is to meet my need. Please help me to read and believe Your creative Word and then trust, depend on, and live by it today and every day. I thank you for it, Amen."

03

Jesus. Everyday Good News

THE SURE WORD OF FAITH

Oliver Nelson, III

My Reflections on "The Sure Word of Faith"

04

Jesus. Everyday Good News

THE FAITH OF JESUS

Oliver Nelson, III

Looking unto Jesus, the author and finisher of our faith, who for the joy set before Him endured the cross, despising the shame, and has sat down at the right hand of the throne of God. (Hebrews 12:2, KJV)

Followers of Jesus Christ talk a lot about *our faith* as if it is *our faith*. Think about faith with me for a few moments. Faith does not begin with us; it is not a product of our *good* hearts. Faith originates with Jesus. Hebrews 12:2 tells us that Jesus is the Author and Finisher of *our* faith (the word *our* was added by the translators and does not even appear in the original Greek language the New Testament was mostly written in). The text should simply read that Jesus is the Author and Finisher of *faith*, period. Faith came forth from His good heart. In other words, Jesus wrote the book on faith, as it were, and He took faith to its ultimate depth. To grow up into the full stature of the character of Christ, we must possess His faith - the faith of Jesus, because it is the only faith acceptable to God.

I think about the life of Jesus. What did Jesus's faith look like when He walked on earth as a man? First, His faith was a faith that did not place primary trust or confidence in men; rather, He trusted all of His ways to God the Father. John, the beloved once declared that even when Jesus was praised by men during His earthly ministry, He did not *commit* Himself to men because He knew what was in man's heart (John 2:24). *Commit* in the original Greek language is the verb form of faith.

We become weak and unstable because too often we place our faith, i.e., our primary trust and confidence, in other humans. When they fail us, we then project their human weaknesses and failings onto God, which leaves us disappointed, to say the least.

THE FAITH OF JESUS

Oliver Nelson, III

Second, the Faith of Jesus never depends upon the arm of the flesh (flesh, meaning relying on our human strength and resources). Jeremiah 17:5 declares that any man who trusts in man and makes flesh his arm is cursed. Although Jesus was God, a Being of limitless power and wisdom when He walked on this planet as a human like us, He declared that of Himself He could "do nothing" (John 5:19). Everything that Jesus did on this earth, every miracle He performed, every transformative word He spoke, was motivated and empowered by God the Father who constantly dwelt in Him and worked through Him (John 14:10). To live lives filled with God's good works and free of selfish motives, like Jesus, we must depend upon God and God alone; allowing Him to work in us as He did in Jesus Christ (Philippians 2:13).

Finally, I believe possessing the Faith of Jesus means we see people as Jesus sees them. Jesus is God, and He knows all things; He can see the future. However, Jesus never conditions His acts of love towards us based on His foreknowledge. When Jesus looks at us, He does not focus His view on our past and present failures, or the future mistakes He knows we will make. Rather, He only sees us as what we might become in Him through the power of His Agape.

A good example of this is found in the story of Paul in Acts 9:1-16. Paul was first called Saul, and he hated followers of Jesus Christ. He was actually on his way to arrest believers when he had a life changing encounter with Christ that left him blind. Jesus had it all planned, in verses 13-15 He instructed Ananias to go to Saul to restore his eyesight. Ananias was scared, as I would have been. He had heard the rumors of the cruelty of Saul. Regardless, Jesus told him to go anyway because Saul has been chosen to represent Him before Gentiles, kings, and the children of Israel. Jesus demonstrated faith in a man who hated Him and was on his way to arrest,

THE FAITH OF JESUS

Oliver Nelson, III

persecute, and maybe even kill those who believed in Him. The faith that Jesus demonstrated toward Saul changed the trajectory of his life. In that messed up, self-righteous, and arrogant man, Jesus saw a friend, ambassador, evangelist, and fearless defender of the gospel of God. Saul turned Paul surrendered to the faith of Jesus in him and the whole world has been so blessed because He did.

When we have the faith of Jesus, we will allow Him full control of our hearts and minds, and He will cause us to treat and view others, including our enemies, as Jesus treats them. Let's not get it twisted; to have the faith that Jesus had, especially in this day and age, requires supernatural strength that only God has. I can testify of that from my own experience, and you probably can also. Thank God He promises that the *"just shall live by His faith"* (Habakkuk 2:4).

As we choose to yield to and cherish His faith, we will experience the message of the Sermon on the Mount, loving our enemies, blessing those who curse us, and doing good to those who hate us (Matthew 5:43-35). The good news is that we don't and can't earn this faith. The faith of Jesus is given to us as a priceless gift. It is the ultimate source of power for every believer in Christ. Through it, we can all access divine love, power, transformation, victory, and reconciliation.

Good News Prayer:

Dearest Jesus, I receive the faith of Jesus into my heart. I can see Your faith working in my life. Help me to put my ultimate trust in the Father and not in any flesh, not even my own. Lead me to view and treat others with Your faith. Do in and through me what only You can do, and cause me to love my neighbors and enemies, to bless those who curse me, and to do good to those who hate me. Amen.

04

Jesus. Everyday Good News

THE FAITH OF JESUS

Oliver Nelson, III

My Reflections on "The Faith of Jesus"

05

Jesus. Everyday Good News

NEVER ALONE -PART 1

Sharon Pergerson

Behold, a virgin shall be with child and shall bring forth a son, and they shall call his name Emmanuel, which being interpreted is, God with us. (Matthew 1:23, KJV)

August 27, 2015, seemed like just another beautiful day, but it wasn't, not after I heard the gut-ripping news over the phone that my husband—my love, my friend, the spiritual leader of our home, and the father of my two precious teenagers—was dead, killed in a plane crash. The kids, screaming, and I, in a state of shock, immediately dropped to our knees and cried out to our God. It felt like we had been thrown out of a spaceship in the darkness of space and were falling and falling with nothing to break our fall. On that devastating day, God had to catch us, pick up the shattered pieces of us, hold us together, and carry us supernaturally through the next painful nights, days, months, and years.

While none of us is ever prepared for the shock of suddenly losing one we dearly love, or for going through any traumatic experience, God is never caught off guard. Unbeknownst to my little family, the truth God emphasized to us from the beginning of that year was exactly what we would need to sustain us through what was to happen that awful day. God understood that because of the level of pain this would inflict upon our family and many others, we needed a deeper, stronger understanding of God's truth, something *made for the occasion* of that dark moment.

We sing about how "God is with us" every Christmas holiday season, yet this underrated truth is more than just a Carole. It is packed with high-dosage, healing power for all of us who have been, or will be, deeply hurt before this life is over. Some weeks before our tragedy someone shared a quote with me from Christian author, Ellen White, a writer whose focus on the beauty and power of

05

Jesus. Everyday Good News

NEVER ALONE - PART 1

Sharon Pergerson

Christ's character has been a blessing to me. This quote, supported by Scripture, shared some therapeutic insights into what "God with us" really means to us personally, and it left an eternal impact on my mind and heart. Here it is:

> *Through all our trials, we have a never-failing Helper. . . . Though now He is hidden from mortal sight, the ear of faith can hear His voice saying, Fear not; I am with you. . . . "I have endured your sorrows, experienced your struggles, encountered your temptations. I know your tears; I also have wept. I know the griefs that lie too deep to be breathed into any human ear. Think not that you are desolate and forsaken. Though your pain touches no responsive chord in any heart on earth, look unto Me, and live [Isaiah 54:10 referenced]. Desire of Ages 442, p. 442.*

I can never explain what this profound quote and all the Bible texts that reiterate it have meant to me over the years of my grieving. We are never alone in anything we go through. God is always with us as a never-failing Helper. In life and especially in those times of terrifying pain that no other human being can understand, the only comfort that can reach that deep is knowing and believing that God Himself is with us. In that dark, lonely space no one else dares enter, God comes and stays as our never-failing, very-present Helper (Psalms 46:1). Glory to God in the Highest. What a God! What a God! Thank you, Jesus.

Good News Prayer

Dear Jesus, may Your truth about being with me as my never-failing Helper, even in my darkest times, comfort and keep me and all your children in our times of need. Thank you for being a God who alone knows and supplies my deepest need.

05

Jesus. Everyday Good News

NEVER ALONE - PART 1

Sharon Pergerson

My Reflections on "Never Alone- Part 1"

06

Jesus. Everyday Good News

NEVER ALONE - PART 2

Sharon Pergerson

Fear thou not; for I am with thee: be not dismayed; for I am thy God: I will strengthen thee; yea, I will help thee; yea, I will uphold thee; yeah, I will uphold thee with the right hand of my righteousness.
(Isaiah 41:10, KJV)

For some people, life has been pretty innocent and safe, and we all thank God for such times. However, I know we all understand that in a minute, things can happen in this life that are so deeply painful that all we can do is sit at the bottom of a dark closet in complete silence. Nobody can go "there" with us and understand how we feel. And, as if those moments of anguish were not enough, life often punches us with additional trauma that further agitates that deep pain.

Alone in our dark corner, we cry out in desperation, "Does God even notice or care about my suffering? Does He know what this pain feels like? The answer is Yes, He knows and cares—and so much more. He says in His Word that He never leaves us nor forsakes us (Hebrews 13:5). He is always with us (Matthew 28:20). Even more than that, He says what is done to us is done to Him (Matthew 25:20). In all our afflictions, He too is afflicted (Isaiah 63:9). "God with us" is His official declaration of His permanent union—with us personally and forever. Wow.

So, as we sit silently, as it were, at the bottom of a dark closet, astounded at all that's happening in our personal lives, shattered communities, divided nation, turbulent world, and bewildered families, know that we are not alone. Our Creator, our Savior, and our never-failing Helper suffers with us. He comes so close; He feels our troubles and gathers our tears unto Himself (Psalm 56:8).

NEVER ALONE-PART 2

Sharon Pergerson

God has mercy on us. What is the ultimate mercy of God? It is that one day, He will avenge all wrongs and make all things new and right. He will take us to the new, safe home He has prepared for all those who long to live with Him. A home that is gun-free, violence-free, racism-free, trauma-free, cop-free, criminal-free, pain-free, poverty-free, separation-free, virus-free, and death-free. Until then, let's let Him keep our hearts singing with hope because Jesus is God with us; we are never alone.

Good News Prayer

Dear Jesus, thank You for holding on to me through every storm thrown against me. Thank you for never leaving me. Thank You for Your promises to carry me safely onto the shores of Heaven, where I will gratefully sing, "the song of Moses, the servant of God, and the song of the Lamb, saying, Great and marvelous are Thy works, Lord God Almighty; just and true are Thy ways, Thou King of saints" (Revelation 15:3).

06

Jesus. Everyday Good News

NEVER ALONE-PART 2

Sharon Pergerson

My Reflections on "Never Alone - Part 2"

07

Jesus. Everyday Good News

ONE WITH US

Oliver Nelson, III

For we have not a high priest which cannot be touched with the feeling of our infirmities; but was in all points tempted like we are, yet without sin. (Hebrews 4:15, KJV)

For me and others, one of our greatest fears is being alone and going through dark times alone. I believe Jesus understood this about us, and so He made Himself one with us. The Bible shares that Jesus, our Sanctifier, and those that are being sanctified (us), are all of one (Hebrews 2:11). Despite our mistakes, our failures, and despite the opinions that others have about us, that same text also makes the remarkable statement that Jesus is not only one with us but that He is also not ashamed to call us His brothers and sisters.

From the descriptions shared in His word, Jesus has connected Himself to us in the most unique and intimate way. He was and remains a partaker of flesh and blood just as we are (Hebrews 2:14). That is to say that even as He sits at the right hand of God the Father, Jesus, who is God, remains a human being. He has connected himself to our human nature, forever. Indeed, He did not take on Himself nature of angels, but that of the seed of Abraham (Hebrews 2:16). As we know, Abraham did not possess a perfect nature; He possessed a nature that drove him to lie on at least two occasions to save himself, dishonoring His God.

No, Jesus absolutely never sinned else He could not be our Savior, and He, like us, would actually need a savior. The Bible record is clear that it was by choice that Jesus took upon Himself the nature of sinful humanity so that He could provide aid, help, or succor to those who are tempted (Hebrews 2:18). There is nothing like having someone who has been in your shoes and found a way out, to help you out of your rut. Jesus intentionally put Himself where we are, but where we failed and gave in to sin, He overcame and won the

ONE WITH US

Oliver Nelson, III

victory over all sin, condemning sin while in our human flesh (Romans 8:1:4). Wow. I have a God who understands my weaknesses and knows how to and will deliver me from them. I am not alone and helpless in my weaknesses.

I am so thankful that we have a God who refused to remain on His heavenly high perch yet lowered Himself to the depths of our sinful condition to save us from that condition. I love the words of Paul in 1 Corinthians 12:9-10 where he reiterates that the power of God's grace works its perfect best for those with weaknesses. As Paul responded, 'If that's the case, I acknowledge and admit my weaknesses so that the delivering, overcoming power of Christ can rest on me.'

Lastly, Jesus has connected himself to our experience. In speaking about his children, of which all of us are, the Bible says that He was afflicted in all our afflictions (Isaiah 63:9). We never go through any experience in this life alone. Jesus has connected himself with us in such a personal way that every heartbreaking experience we go through in this life, He also feels and experiences. He reminds us of His connection with us in our experience so that we might have the boldness to come before His throne of grace to obtain mercy to help us in our time of need (Hebrews 4:16).

Good News Prayer

Dear Jesus, I cannot even begin to tell You what it means to me to know that You have made yourself one with me, that You have connected yourself to me so that You can help me in every area of my messed-up life and be with me in every experience I go through. I am never alone, and I have all that I need. Thank you, Jesus.

07

Jesus. Everyday Good News

ONE WITH US

Oliver Nelson, III

My Reflections on "One with Us"

08

Jesus. Everyday Good News

THE FORGOTTEN MIRACLE

Sharon Pergerson

Thanks be unto God for His unspeakable gift.
(2 Corinthians 9:15, KJV)

Your day may have started beautifully, but by the end of it, you may have lost your husband, wife, child, mother, father, best friend, or someone else close to your heart. Death is not natural to God's creation, so you are never really prepared, and it never feels "ok." However, sudden death takes things to an even darker, cruel level. You, like me, may have asked God why He would allow such a horrible thing to happen to His child, His servant, one who loved Him so much and just wanted to serve Him and bless others. You may have asked why God hadn't performed a miracle for your loved one and spared his or her life as He had done so many times before and for so many others.

We all love a testimony that ends with a supernatural miracle of God, like a near-death encounter or healing from a fatal disease. In my personal experience, as I pondered my own husband's apparent "no miracle" experience, I believe the Holy Spirit showed me that God had performed a miracle for my husband. *The Forgotten Miracle*, as I call it, is that God made death a sleep from which He will awaken all.

My husband, like all the rest of us, was a sinner. *"The wages of sin is death; but the gift of God is eternal life through Jesus Christ our Lord."* (Romans 6:23). I believe the death Paul refers to here is not the first death of the grave that we experience as a result of our mortality. It is the "second death" which is placed in contrast to eternal life. That's the death my husband and all of us deserve. However, as a result of the actions of Jesus Christ toward the whole world, all who go into the grave, both the just and unjust, will awaken from the first death. Scripture says that *"for as in Adam all die, even so in Christ shall all be made alive"* (1 Corinthians 15:32). Some will eventually awake to face everlasting death, per their choice. The good news is that those who have received Jesus Christ as the Lord and Savior of their lives will awaken to face everlasting life, never having to taste eternal death, which is goodbye to life, forever. And, lest we forget, that gift of everlasting life is the everlasting life of a Person, Jesus Christ. 1 John 5:11-12 tells us that God put it on record that when we have received and hold on to His Son, Jesus Christ, we have His (Jesus's) everlasting life now. Wow, Hallelujah.

Thus, as we abide in Christ and He in us, the temporary sleep of death may claim us, or our loved ones, but it cannot rob us of God's miracle to us; eternal death will never touch us. That much-forgotten miracle cost Heaven everything to grant to us. No wonder Jesus must have shouted victoriously, "*...Death is swallowed up in victory. O death, where is thy sting? O grave where is your victory?*" (1 Corinthians 15:54-55, KJV). Now Jesus holds the keys of death and hell (Revelation 1:18). He conquered death and the grave so that you and I will one day soon be forever done with fear, separation, and pain.

That's wonderful, good news that all who have experienced loss need to hear every day. Meanwhile, until that great getting up morning, Jesus joins us in our suffering. He feels our loss, for it is His loss also. He sticks with us, as is said, like white on rice. Now, because of the unspeakable gift of God's forgotten miracle, given to us in Jesus Christ, our souls may be filled with peace, anticipation, and rejoicing. Even as we grieve, Jesus's words to Mary at the loss of her brother are for all of us, He says to us, *"I am the resurrection, and the life: he that believeth in me, though he were dead, yet shall he live* (John 11:25, KJV). May these words and thoughts encourage us all (1 Thessalonians 4:16-18).

08

Jesus. Everyday Good News

THE FORGOTTEN MIRACLE

Sharon Pergerson

Everyday Good News Prayer

Thank you, God, for your forgotten miracle. Thank you for sticking with me on this painful journey through the valley of the shadow of death. Thank you that with you I need fear no evil for You are with me (Psalms 23). Help me to cherish all your priceless gift to me and hold on to Jesus by faith until my hope becomes sight, soon and very soon. Amen.

08

Jesus. Everyday Good News

THE FORGOTTEN MIRACLE

Sharon Pergerson

My Reflections on "The Forgotten Miracle"

09

Jesus. Everyday Good News

SEEKING RIGHTEOUSNESS

Oliver Nelson, III

Thy righteousness also, O God, is very high, Who hast done great things: O God, who is like unto thee (Psalms 71:19, KJV).

We often hear the word *righteousness* used during religious conversations; however, it is not often that we look into its biblical description. In the word itself, *righteousness*, I saw *right*, and it made me nervous. Outside of Christ, I knew there was nothing *right* about me, or any of us for that matter. In Psalms 71:19, David, the psalmist, posed a grand question, God, who is like you, who has righteousness that reaches Your level? Then, in Psalms 145:17, David shared that God is righteous and holy in everything He does. In Psalms 119:172 he explained that God's commandments are righteousness. Righteousness, then, is God's high standard of what is right and correct based on His character and as described by His commandments.

What are those commandments? One popular summary of them is found in Exodus 20. There, God first reminded his people of how He miraculously delivered them from Egypt, and due to that, He stated that they were to uphold certain behaviors like worshiping Him only, remembering His Sabbath, and honoring their fathers and mothers; and they were to refrain from other behaviors such as murder, stealing, lying, and committing adultery, to name a few. Taking those statements at face value, for us to be righteous would mean not doing, or doing, the things He listed. It's just a list of 10 things we can all do easily, can't we? The ancient Israelites agreed to that list in Exodus 24:7 and even today there are some who walk around with that same checklist in their back pocket believing they are successfully "doing" God's commandments.

However, Jesus seemed to view righteousness and God's law a lot more deeply. In Matthew 19:16-22, Jesus was confronted by a rich young ruler who called Him good and asked Him what good thing he should do to be saved. Jesus responded by first asking what he meant by calling Him good. Jesus may have been trying to make sure the young man understood that there are levels of *good(*ness) or, righteousness (see Matthew 5:20). However, if he meant "good" as in perfect- without sin all the time (perfect righteousness), only God qualifies, and Jesus is God. Jesus then strategically answered this young man's question by telling him that if he wanted to enter heaven, he must keep the commandments. When the young man asked which ones, Jesus named them for him in verses 18-19. The young man responded that he had been keeping those all his life and asked what else he was missing.

Let's pause before we go thinking this young man was just being prideful, arrogant, and self-righteous. In actuality, he was asking the right question, the most serious question we should all be asking and making sure we know the answer to: "What does God require from us to qualify us for attaining eternal life?" This young man had lived morally and respectably all his life, made all the right decisions that led to his success and wealth, and was spiritual and concerned about his salvation. From human eyes, he should have been at the front of the line for attaining eternal life. Certainly, he was the cream of the crop.

However, for him to come to Jesus with a resume like that and ask that question makes me know he was desperate; he knew something was not right and that his good(ness) was not enough to save him. There he was doing all the "right" things, yet he had no peace and no assurance of his eternal future. Something serious was missing in His life and he could no longer afford to ignore it. It must have pained Jesus to show this rich young man the truth about his good(ness). He knew His answer to the young man would be the turning point in

SEEKING RIGHTEOUSNESS

Oliver Nelson, III

his life and destiny. Jesus wanted peace and eternal salvation for him; He had come from Heaven to give that to him. With a heart filled with love and sympathy, Jesus told him to go and sell everything he owned and distribute the proceeds to the poor in exchange for the wealth of Heaven. Then He invited him to come and follow Him. Verse 22 tells us that when the young man heard those words, he left saddened and disappointed because of his vast riches and wealth. Sadly, Jesus turned and told his disciples how impossible it was for a rich man to be saved; in fact, it was easier for a camel to go through the eye of a needle than for a rich man to get into heaven. This response stunned the disciples and left them wondering who then could make it into heaven. If rich good doers didn't qualify, who did? What chance did they or anyone else have? Jesus lovingly looked at them and told them that what was impossible for sinful humans to do (to be saved) is possible with God.

Jesus can see beyond the surface of sinful human *good(*ness), also called self-righteousness. He could see that deep down inside, that rich young man cherished his possessions and his goodness more than He loved God. His riches and possessions were his god. He had broken God's command of loving the Lord with all of his heart, mind, and soul, and loving others as he loved himself (Matthew 22:37-40). Thus, his right doing, his goodness, or his self-righteousness, masked a deeper defect. This young man's righteousness may have appeared honorable on the surface, but it fell short of reaching the high standard of God's character, making it not good enough to quality him to live forever. God cannot be fooled, no one can fake it into heaven. God views sinful human *good*(ness), or self- righteousness as filthy rags that He will not and cannot accept as a qualifier for entrance into heaven (Isaiah 64:6; Romans 3:10). Honestly, God nor us, wants any hint of selfishness in heaven. That's what is messing up

SEEKING RIGHTEOUSNESS

Oliver Nelson, III

our world now. The story of the rich young man who came to Jesus with that critical question shares a powerful truth that's hard for *rich* sinners to bear. The central point of this story was not about the physically wealthy not getting into heaven (there will be countless numbers of them there); it is about the importance of understanding the standard that must be met for anyone to be saved. Our human goodness or self-righteousness- too often our *riches-* is not good enough and never will be to qualify us to be saved. Why? because it's always contaminated with impure, selfish motives that defy the commands and character of God. Jesus said the qualification for heaven is to keep God's commandments. This means being right and doing the right thing, for the right reasons... from pure, unselfish motives... ALL the time- from the cradle to the grave! That's perfect righteousness. Whether we like it or not, this disqualifies all of us (James 2:10). Perfect righteousness is absolutely impossible for sinful, broken human beings like you and me!

Why, then, would God ask us to do something He knows is impossible for us to do? Firstly, God could command the impossible because He was going to fulfill it in Christ. 1 Corinthians 1:30 shared that God made Jesus Christ to be our righteousness and everything we need. God knew the effect of sin on us, and He never meant for us to believe we could ever do any *good* thing that would qualify us for heaven. All that Jesus did when He came to earth as one of us, He did perfectly. He lived a perfect life, without any sin (2 Corinthians 5:21). By His death on the cross He took our record as His and secured the right to give us His record of perfect righteousness in exchange (Romans 5:17-21). As long as we receive Christ into our hearts and stay connected to Him, His record of perfect righteousness remains ours, as does His eternal life (1 John 5:11-12).

SEEKING RIGHTEOUSNESS

Oliver Nelson, III

Secondly, as we abide in Him and He in us, He lives out His life of righteousness in our lives so that we become more and more like Him (see John 15:4-5; Gal. 5:22; and Ephesians 5:9). Then, as we seek His righteousness in our personal experience, we begin to find that the self-righteous things we used think and do, we do them no more, and the things that are impossible for us to do (works of perfect righteousness), are being done in our lives, by Jesus Christ, through the Holy Spirit. Notice the following Bible verses:

- *For it is God, which worketh in you both to will and to do of His good pleasure (Philippians 2:13, KJV).*
- *Being confident of this very thing, that He which hath begun a good work in you will perform it until the day of Jesus Christ: (Philippians 1:6, KJV).*
- *Verily, verily, I say unto you, He that believeth on me, the works that I do shall he do also; and greater works than these shall he do; because I go unto my Father (John 14:12).*

Every believer in Jesus Christ who trusts in His righteousness and submits to its power by faith is fully qualified for eternal life. In Jesus, they have perfect righteousness—God's ultimate standard of right-doing based on His character, revealed through His commandments, and fulfilled in the actions of His Son, Jesus. Praise God!

Everyday Good News Prayer

Dearest Father, though painful to admit, thank you for clearing my vision of me and my self-righteous "riches". Thank you for attaining for me what I could never attain for myself. Thank You for taking my messed-up record to the cross and giving me Your perfect record of righteousness. By faith, I submit to its transformative power. In Jesus's name, amen.

09

Jesus. Everyday Good News

SEEKING RIGHTEOUSNESS

Oliver Nelson, III

My Reflections on "Seeking Righteousness"

10

Jesus. Everyday Good News

THE COMPASSIONATE FATHER

Chernae Saka

Come now, and let us reason together, saith the Lord: though your sins be as scarlet, they shall be as white as snow; though they be red like crimson, they shall be as wool. (Isaiah 1:18, KJV)

I recently saw a video clip of a police officer attempting to arrest a 14-year-old young man. The kid had a gun in his hand, having just fatally wounded his mother. Although the police officer knew what he had done, he could have been aggressive, escalating the situation and potentially shooting and killing the young man. However, the officer didn't do that. He pleaded with the young man and told him, "Hey, we know what has happened, but this does not have to be your fate, nor does it have to define you."

He skillfully instructed the young man to put down the gun, come to the grassy area, and lie down, and he would arrest him. The young man clung to the officer's every word, trusting the officer would not misstep...and the officer didn't. The young man was finally arrested and taken into custody. The police officer acted with compassion and empathy by not allowing the bad situation to worsen.

God is a compassionate, loving Father, and in that particular instance, that police officer was acting as the Father. Similarly, in Isa. 1:18, God calls out to us to come to Him, and then He pleads, "Let us reason together". This text is so sweet! It is a picture of God the Father gently beckoning his child to open up in conversation and connectivity. Despite our sins against God, He doesn't hold us at arms' length. He desires for us to reason and commune with Him. It is through that communion with Him that we are changed. It's important to note who it is who promises to change our sins from red to white; this promise comes from God. He is saying don't despair over your sins, struggles, and entanglements; come to Me

THE COMPASSIONATE FATHER

Chernae Saka

and let us reason together. Rather than disconnecting from us because of our sins, God invites us to come closer, to dialogue with Him, and in doing so, we will be cleansed and find rest for our sin-weary souls (Matthew 11:28).

You may be wondering what the compassionate Father has to do with Jesus being our everyday good news. Jesus Himself explained it by indicating that He and the Father are One (John 10:30). Their nature is the same. They have the same heart of peace, grace, and love toward all their children (2 John 1:3). Jesus even said that when we see Him, we see the Father (John 14:9). He also said that whatever we saw Him do, was the Father doing it in and through Him (John 14:10). Jesus's whole life was a reflection of the compassionate heart and will of God, the Father. Together, they are on our side. Together, they are for us.

Sometimes, we are tempted to believe that Jesus is for us, but we are not so sure about how God the Father feels about us. We may even believe that Jesus is somewhere begging the Father to have compassion on us and not destroy us. No, no, no. Whatever we see in Jesus is God's will toward us. God the Father directed this whole plan to reach and save us. At the cross, God was in or together with Christ in reconciling the world back to Himself (2 Corinthians 5:19). God the Father's compassion is plastered all over the accomplishments of Jesus, our everyday good news.

Everyday Good News Prayer

Dear Father in Heaven, may I not fall prey to the enemy's devices in keeping me away from You. Despite the messes I find myself in, Lord, may I press on and come to You because I know through that reasoning and communicating with You that I will be made clean and find rest. Thank You, Amen!

10

Jesus. Everyday Good News

THE COMPASSIONATE FATHER

Chernae Saka

My Reflections on "The Compassionate Father"

11

Jesus. Everyday Good News

THE NEARNESS OF OUR SAVIOR

Chernae Saka

In all their affliction he was afflicted, and the angel of his presence saved them; in his love and his pity he redeemed them; he lifted them up and carried them all the days of old. (Isaiah 63:9, KJV)

There is an old hymn by Ruth Caye Jones that goes like this:

"In times like these, you need a Savior, In times like these you need an anchor; Be very sure, be very sure, Your anchor holds and grips the Solid Rock! This Rock is Jesus, Yes He's the One, This Rock is Jesus, the only One; Be very sure, be very sure, your anchor holds and grips the Solid Rock!"

This hymn has proven true so many times in my life. There comes a point in our lives where we need more than just motivational speeches, words of affirmation, or positive vibes. We need a Savior! We need One who is familiar with the terrain and more than willing to save and deliver us. Isaiah 63:9 reminds us that in all our afflictions, He was afflicted, meaning that in all our sorrows, sufferings, discouragements, disappointments, and heartbreaks, Jesus Himself experiences because He has connected Himself as us and with us.

It is because of His love that we are saved and redeemed. His is not a picture of a lifeguard who sits on his high tower, examining the situation, calling out commands to cease from horseplay, and occasionally throwing out a buoy as he pulls the endangered to safety. No! His is a picture of a Savior who jumps into the murky, dangerous river, firmly grabs hold of you and me, and swims us to safety. Our Savior, Jesus Christ, is a very present help in our time of need. He does not keep a distance but comes ever so near to us, especially in the times of our affliction.

11

Jesus. Everyday Good News

THE NEARNESS OF OUR SAVIOR

Chernae Saka

Everyday Good News Prayer

Heavenly Father, I thank you for Jesus. I thank you for loving me and staying ever near me. Despite my circumstances, you are always with me. It is only because of your love that in Christ I am saved and redeemed, and for that, Father, I say thank You! Amen.

11

Jesus. Everyday Good News

THE NEARNESS OF OUR SAVIOR

Chernae Saka

My Reflections on "The Nearness of Our Savior"

12

Jesus. Everyday Good News

EAGLE VISION

Sharon Pergerson

I will instruct thee and teach thee in the way which thou shalt go: I will guide thee with Mine eye. (Psalms 32:8, KJV)

The next three "*thoughts*" continue to explore the character of Jesus through the lens of nature, God's second lesson book. Although affected by sin, nature still reveals the glory and character of Jesus. I hope these reflections are a blessing to all who read and hear them.

When my children were little, they were obsessed with studying animals and nature. My eight-year-old son considered himself the resident expert on all things related to animals. Sadly, as we grow older, the cares of life often rob us of the time needed to invest in such noble studies. A man named Job, in Job 12:7-10, told his friends to do something he felt was very important: to observe what God's creation taught them about Him. I accepted Job's challenge by researching what the eagle had to teach me about God. It had much to "say," starting with its vision.

An eagle's vision is among the strongest of all of God's creatures; it is 4 to 8 times stronger than perfect human vision. An eagle can see miles away and detect what other birds do not, such as a tiny lizard on a rock from a thousand feet up or the movement of a fish underwater. That's like seeing an ant crawling on the ground from the roof of a 10-story building. When an eagle sees its chosen target, it narrows its focus and sets out to catch it. Its vision remains fixed solely on its target, regardless of obstacles. An eagle will only divert its focus once it has secured its prey. Even when an eagle spots a large group of animals, it targets one and goes for it, leaving the others behind.

I had long believed that the primary purpose of creation was for

12 Jesus. Everyday Good News

EAGLE VISION

Sharon Pergerson

man's enjoyment and delight. I was very wrong. I believe the primary purpose of creation is to reveal the character of Jesus Christ: His love, His faithfulness, and His power—so that we can confidently put our full trust in Him. Thus, an eagle's vision teaches us about Christ's keen eyesight, which entails His loving, watchful care over us, His power, and His faithfulness over all His creation. Notice these Bible verses:

- *For the eyes of the LORD run to and fro throughout the whole earth, to show Himself strong on behalf of them whose heart is perfect toward Him" (2 Chronicles 16:9, KJV).*
- *For His eyes are upon the ways of man, and He sees all his goings" (Job 34:21, KJV).*
- *Behold, the eye of the LORD is upon them that fear Him, upon them that hope in His mercy" (Psalms 33:18, KJV)*

While sin has corrupted the purpose of the eagle's vision, we can still use it to better understand how Christ sees His children among the captives of Satan. He narrows His focus to all those who desire to be set free from the clutches of evil. Jesus came to set the captives free, for *"if the Son therefore shall make you free, ye shall be free indeed"* (John 8:36, KJV).

No matter the obstacle, Christ will not remove His focus from us until He has us securely in His arms and safe in the kingdom of heaven. Like Paul on the road to Damascus, like Zacchaeus in the branches of a tree, like Mary caught in adultery, like the thief at his end on the cross, or like me lost in trying to figure life out, no matter how many distractions there are, Christ is well able to save to the uttermost every sinner who responds to His powerful "eyes" of love and faith upon them (Hebrews 7:25).

Everyday Good News Prayer

Thank You, Jesus, for Your watchful, powerful eyes over me to rescue and save me to the uttermost. I come to You, I receive You, and I trust my all to You. In Jesus's name, amen.

12

Jesus. Everyday Good News

EAGLE VISION

Sharon Pergerson

My Reflections on "Eagle Vision"

13

Jesus. Everyday Good News

EAGLE GRIP

Sharon Pergerson

Fear not, for I am with you; Be not dismayed, for I am your God. I will strengthen you, Yes, I will help you, I will uphold you with My righteous right hand. (Isaiah 41:10, NKJV)

The lessons I've learned from the eagle was the therapy my spiritual walk desperately needed. I couldn't wait for my next study about the strength of an eagle's grip. No matter the obstacle, an eagle will not remove his focus from his target until he grabs it with his powerful talons. Just looking at those talons and seeing how they worked left me speechless. I could see the power, a picture that needs absolutely nothing to describe it. Their "point" is very clear.

Talons are so strong that it is extremely difficult for an eagle to lose what it carries. Their grip is about 10 times stronger than the human hand, and they can carry something four times their weight. The strength of those talons comes from the muscles in the eagle's legs, which, when contracted, clamp the tendons in the lower legs and toes down, closing all the talons together in a vice-like grip that only those willing to rip their life apart can escape.

We know that because of sin, talons are now used to destroy life for survival purposes; however, I believe talons were designed by God to carry something securely through the air, and by faith, we can still learn the primary lessons of an eagle's grip. To me, an eagle's talons are a reminder of Christ's powerful ability to not only find and free every heart who is willing from the clutches of Satan, but also to hold on to us with His mighty strength and safely carry us to where He has promised us. He has promised this to all, regardless of the dangerous obstacles in His path. It is His power alone that can keep us and save us. His Word to us is emphatically clear, *"neither is there salvation in any other: for there is none other name under heaven given among men, whereby we must be saved."* (Acts 4:12, KJV).

13

Jesus. Everyday Good News

EAGLE GRIP

Sharon Pergerson

Sadly, for whatever reason, we stumble at the idea of Christ's power alone being enough to save us completely. Too often, we feel we must help Him save us. In fact, some of us believe it's a fifty-fifty partnership endeavor. That must be pretty insulting to God. There's a reason Job, in Job 12:7-10, tells us to ask the earth, the birds, and the fish about the character of God—about His love, His faith, and His power. Did you notice that Job doesn't even mention man, God's crowning act of creation, in that list? We struggle to surrender to the fact that we can do nothing without Him. Perhaps we all need to hang a close-up picture of an eagle's talons in our homes and hearts to look at when we find unbelief, like cancer cells, gaining ground in our hearts, minds, and experiences, robbing us of the peace that comes through trusting God's Word about the power of His Son. God knows that unbelief is the besetting sin of His children. Yet still, His heart is full of love, faith, and compassion. To us, He gives this healing reminder:

> *"The Father loveth the Son and hath given all things into His hand. All that the Father giveth Me shall come to Me, and I will in no wise cast out. For I came down from heaven, not to do mine own will, but the will of Him that sent Me. And this is the Father's will which hath sent Me, that of all He hath given Me I should lose nothing but raise it again at the last day. And this is the will of Him that sent me, that every one that seeth the Son, and believeth in Him, may have everlasting life: and I will raise him at the last day. (John 6:35, 37-40, KJV).*

Everyday Good News Prayer

Join me with Jude (24) in confidently praying this promise, "Now unto Him who can keep you (say me) from falling, and to present you (say me) faultless before the presence of His glory with exceeding joy, to the only wise God our Saviour, be glory and majesty, dominion and power, both now and forever." I claim this in Jesus's name, amen.

13

Jesus. Everyday Good News

EAGLE GRIP

Sharon Pergerson

My Reflections on "Eagle Grip"

14

Jesus. Everyday Good News

EAGLE WINGS

Sharon Pergerson

How excellent is Thy lovingkindness, O God! Therefore the children of men put their trust under the shadow of Thy wings. (Psalms 36:7, KJV)

Just when I thought the lessons the eagle had taught me couldn't get any sweeter, he spread his wings. Eagles are among the most majestic flying creatures in the world. An eagle has a wingspan that can grow to a little over 8 feet long. Its 7000 feathers weigh about twice as much as its skeleton. During storms and strong winds, when other birds disappear in fear, an eagle is strong enough to spread its wings and soar with the aid of strong winds, which force it higher and higher through and above the storm.

An eagle doesn't just fly haphazardly, though; it has an inborn ability to sense the motion of air currents. This magnificent creature often won't budge until the right breeze comes along. When it does, the eagle just lets go. It flaps its wings a few times, but mostly, the eagle just lets go and is borne upward by the force of the wind. An eagle can soar like that using thermal currents of air. These warm air patterns are created by the surrounding terrain. Thus, it can simply spread its wings and tail feathers and let the wind carry it to new heights; then, it glides down to catch another upward thermal. Soaring saves an eagle energy because it does not have to flap its wings as often.

While I was thinking that God would give me wings to fly like that, Mr. Eagle busted my bubble. An eagle's wings are to teach us that we are to place our trust in the power of God's wings. It is under His wings that we are to abide, there we are safe, there our confidence is to be, and there we are to remain connected to Him. What are God's wings? I believe they are His all-encompassing character of love and faith, as seen in Christ, which covers all our needs.

14

EAGLE WINGS

Sharon Pergerson

Psalms 91, especially verse 4 reads, *"He shall cover thee with His feathers, and under His wings shalt thou trust* (KJV)..." We can trust in His love and faith, in us. Talk about supplying our need, Philippians 4:19 reminds us that *"My God shall supply all your need according to His riches in glory by Christ Jesus,"* and 1 Corinthians 1:30 reminds us *"but of Him are ye in Christ Jesus, who of God is made unto to us wisdom, and righteousness, and sanctification, and redemption"* (KJV). I love the imagery of God's Words to the ancient children of Israel, *"Ye have seen what I did unto the Egyptians, and how I bare you on eagle's wings, and brought you unto Myself"* (Exodus 19:4, KJV).

It will never be our supposed goodness or strength that leads God to love, bless, and save us. It has always been the strength of God's love for us and His faith in us that led Him to do all He has done for us, in Jesus Christ. It is that same character that, in due time, led Christ to face and go through the greatest storm and danger ever, becoming sin for us and paying the penalty for the death we should have experienced alone and never returned from. That same character has provided a way for us, in Jesus Christ, to be carried safely through every storm of life until, at last, one day soon, we are safe in the clear atmosphere of eternal life: to live with Him forever. Thank You, Jesus.

Everyday Good News Prayer

Sing with me or listen to the words of William Cushing's song:

"Under His Wings, I am safely abiding, though the night deepens and tempests are wild. Still, I can trust Him, I know He will keep me; He has redeemed me and I am His child. Under His wings, under His wings, Who from His love can sever? Under His wings, my soul shall abide, Safely abide forever." Thank You Jesus, amen.

14

Jesus. Everyday Good News

EAGLE WINGS

Sharon Pergerson

My Reflections on "Eagle Wings"

15

Jesus. Everyday Good News

GOD IS NOT WILLING...

Chernae Saka

The Lord is not slack concerning His promises, as some men count slackness: but is longsuffering to us-ward, not willing that any should perish, but that all should come to repentance. (2 Peter 3:9, KJV)

In my quiet moments, as I thought about the above text, I looked up the words *"longsuffering"* and *"not willing."* According to Strong's Concordance, the word *'longsuffering'* means not losing heart, persevering patiently and bravely, enduring misfortunes and troubles, being patient in bearing the offenses and injuries of others, and being mild and slow in avenging. The expression, *not willing,* underscores that Jesus exhausted Himself to save us. His deliberate will for us is to completely save all of us, in every sense of the word. We see this in the three parables in Luke 15: the lost sheep, the coin, and the son. All three parables share the theme of something or someone being lost, a search ensuing for it or them, and it or them being found again.

These parables reveal the heart, will, and determination of Jesus to save us. A man with 100 sheep notices that one is missing. Despite still having 99 sheep left, at great risk, the man leaves the 99 to search for one missing sheep. After finding the lost sheep, he rejoices and celebrates its recovery with friends and neighbors (Luke 15:3-7). The parable of the lost coin in verses 8-10 follows a similar pattern.

In verses 13-32, the parable of the lost son adds another dimension of portraying the unified will of our Heavenly Father in our salvation. The father runs to meet the returning son, even in the face of the older brother's resistance. The father doesn't brush off the response from the older brother, nor does he leave him where he is. We see that the father even goes after the older brother and begs him to join the celebration. God is not a respecter of persons.

15

Jesus. Everyday Good News

GOD IS NOT WILLING...

Chernae Saka

He is true to His Word. He was in Christ reconciling the world to Himself (2 Corinthians 5:19). Jesus is not willing that anyone perish. This deliberate "not willing" drive is also evident in the exchange between Christ and Abraham in Genesis 18:23-33. God revealed His intention to destroy Sodom and Gomorrah due to their great sin. Abraham protested, asking God if He would destroy the righteous along with the wicked. God assured Abraham that He wouldn't, so Abraham bargained with God on the number of righteous people needed to save the city. He discovered that even if only one righteous person existed, God would still spare the cities.

Our Heavenly Father's love, as demonstrated in Jesus Christ, is so lavish that He is 'not willing' that anyone be lost, meaning He has done and will do everything possible to save us. Jesus's lament for Jerusalem in Luke 13:34 reflects Jesus's longing to guard, protect, and save us, akin to a hen caring for her chicks. Sadly, despite making His will abundantly clear, Jesus will not force us to return to Him when He comes searching for us. Salvation is an invitation, and God patiently awaits our response.

Everyday Good News Prayer

Dear Heavenly Father, I thank You for loving me with such great love that You are not willing that I nor any other soul be lost. In Jesus Christ, You have truly lavished me with all I need to be saved past, present, and future. Lord, help me acknowledge this every day and hold this truth deep in my heart so that it may lead me to repentance. I love You, Lord. In Jesus's name, amen!

15

Jesus. Everyday Good News

GOD IS NOT WILLING...

Chernae Saka

My Reflections on "God is Not Willing"

16

Jesus. Everyday Good News

EVEN ME - PART 1

Chernae Saka

If I ascend up into heaven, thou art there: if I make my bed in hell, behold, thou art there. (Psalm 139:8, KJV)

Though we know that God's love is unconditional, changeless, and selfless, have you ever wondered how God feels toward us when we are in blatant sin? Imagine lying on the clinic table having an abortion or in the very midst of having an affair with another woman's husband. How about stealing to support a drug addiction or committing murder? Most of us would probably say, "Oh, I would never do that." We might even judge the person thus engaged harshly. However, there is a wise quote, "Never say never," but for the grace of God, we do not know what we would or would not do if we found ourselves in such predicaments.

The good news is that God has promised never to leave nor forsake us (Deuteronomy 31:6). In this truth, we can rest assured. However, how does God feel about His children who may have gotten themselves entangled in precarious circumstances? Fear, guilt, and misunderstandings cause us to wonder. That wondering can be strong and very present after the committed acts, and if not treated correctly, several things may result, such as lifelong guilt, apathy, suicide, or repentance and reconciliation.

We see a few examples of this in the contrasting stories of Judas and Peter. Judas conspired and led out in the setup to have Jesus crucified. Meanwhile Peter (who at Jesus's most vulnerable moment, swore and cursed at those who knew he was in association with Jesus), ultimately denied Jesus. I believe these two acts shook both disciples to the core. It's that feeling and awareness that you have completely violated everything God stands for; where you find yourself on the outside where it is truly cold and there is a great sense of failure and unworthiness.

16

Jesus. Everyday Good News

EVEN ME - PART 1

Chernae Saka

How did Jesus react to these two disciples? In reference to Judas, Matthew 26:50 says, "*but Jesus said to him, Friend, why have you come?*" Jesus still considered Judas a friend. He did not condemn him nor shun him. In a beautiful book on the life of Christ, called *The Desire of Ages*, the author, Ellen White, commented on this story:

> *"The Saviour did not reproach His betrayer. He knew that Judas did not repent; his confession was forced from his guilty soul by an awful sense of condemnation and a looking for of judgment, but he felt no deep heartbreaking grief that he had betrayed the spotless Son of God and denied the Holy One of Israel. Yet Jesus spoke no word of condemnation. He looked pityingly upon Judas and said, for this hour came I into the world" (p. 766).*

Despite Jesus' merciful response, Judas' refusal to repent of his cruel betrayal was his rejection of the Son of God as his Savior. Instead of heeding the examples of countless individuals who came to Jesus during his earthly ministry in repentance or for healing from various degrees of sickness. From his response, Judas resolved within himself that he would rather take his own life than repent and/or face the consequences of his actions. What a tragedy; may this not be our recourse, for where there is life, there is hope in Christ.

In contrast, consider David's response during his "fall" in Psalm 139:1-6:

> *"O Lord, you have searched me and known me! You know when I sit down and when I rise up; you discern my thoughts from afar. You search out my path and my lying down and are acquainted with all my ways. Even before a word is on my tongue, behold, O Lord, you know it altogether. You hem me in, behind and before, and lay your hand upon me. Such knowledge is too wonderful for me; it is high; I cannot attain it.*

16

Jesus. Everyday Good News

EVEN ME - PART 1

Chernae Saka

Where shall I go from your Spirit? Or where shall I flee from your presence? If I ascend to heaven, you are there! If I make my bed in hell, you are there! If I take the wings of the morning and dwell in the uttermost parts of the sea, even there your hand shall lead me, and your right hand shall hold me. If I say, "Surely the darkness shall cover me, and the light about me be night," even the darkness is not dark to you; the night is bright as the day, for darkness is as light with you" (KJV).

David realized that despite his shortcomings, God was always with him. David knew that God was there to cleanse, aid, lead, guide, and restore him. Thus, he could go to God in confession and repentance. Tomorrow, we will see how God responded to Peter.

Everyday Good News Prayer

Dearest Heavenly Father, I know the enemy comes to steal, kill, and destroy, but You came that I may have life and have it more abundantly. Amid my weaknesses, may I see that You did not wait for me to get things right to die for me, but that You loved me so much that You died while I was in sin. Lord may the depth of Your demonstrated love lead me to repentance. May I believe that nothing I have done or will do is out of your scope of forgiveness and reconciliation. Thank you, Lord. Amen!

16

Jesus. Everyday Good News

EVEN ME - PART 1

Chernae Saka

My Reflections on "Even Me Lord- Part 1"

17

Jesus. Everyday Good News

EVEN ME - PART 2

Chernae Saka

Or despisest thou the riches of his goodness and forbearance and longsuffering; not knowing that the goodness of God leadeth thee to repentance? (Romans 2:4, KJV)

The feeling of betrayal at the hands of a close relative, friend, or loved one is a very unnerving experience as it is rooted in deception. You would never think that the one you truly cared for would betray your trust in such a way that it cost you everything, especially when you needed them the most. Yesterday, we discussed Judas, and today, we will look at Peter.

How did Jesus respond to Peter? Jesus was aware that Peter was going to deny Him three times. He had warned him of it (Matthew 26:34), so this denial did not catch Jesus off guard. In fact, neither did Judas' betrayal. I believe Jesus saw, heard, and, in sorrow born of love, gazed at Peter in that dark hour. Maybe the look of love and mercy in Jesus's eyes made Peter remember the words He had spoken to him in the upper chamber after his zealous assertion, *"Though all men shall be offended because of Thee, I will never be offended" (Matthew 26:33, KJV).*

Peter had denied his Lord, even with cursing and swearing, but I believe, as other writers, that the look from Jesus's eyes melted Peter's guilt-ridden heart and saved him from destroying himself. He probably wept bitterly, and we know he repented of his great sin, and we can venture to say it was probably during that dark time that Peter was converted and then prepared to strengthen his fellow believers.

Despite this painful hiccup, Peter became a faithful apostle of Jesus Christ. Before Jesus's crucifixion, Peter confessed that He was the Christ at least three times. When others left from following Jesus, He asked His disciples if they would also leave from following Him,

17

Jesus. Everyday Good News

EVEN ME - PART 2

Chernae Saka

"Then Simon Peter answered Him, Lord, to whom shall we go? Thou hast the words of eternal life. And we believe and are sure that thou art Christ, the Son of the living God" (John 6:68-69, KJV).

Regardless of how badly he messed up, Peter realized there was no hope or life outside of Christ. In his moments of desperation, his only assurance was the love he saw in the eyes of Jesus Christ and the prayer he remembered Jesus praying for him in Luke 22:31-32. With this realization, Peter was able to choose life over death and hope over despair. In our weaknesses and failures, may we choose Christ. He is not surprised or taken aback by our actions and decisions that go against His will. He is praying for us, and His hand is still outstretched, longing to take us back.

Peter's story is my story. I had been in church all my life. My father is a Pastor, so I inherited the title "PK" – pastor's kid. I lived a sheltered life. I knew right from wrong as spelled out in the 10 commandments. I was very proud of this knowledge, yet I did not have an actual relationship with Jesus. I remember one of the times, like Peter, I failed my Savior and completely violated His commands. Afterward, I immediately feared for my life, thinking that God was going to strike me down that day (though that is not His character). I was actually shocked that God spared my life.

Months and years later, I began to notice the intentional mercy and kindness God kept showing me. He was wooing me unto Himself, just like a young man striving to win the heart of a young lady. Through the sermons I listened to at church, God brought me to a point, much like a young man ready to propose to a young lady. Each message brought about a conviction that was so strong and pointed, I knew that the Holy Spirit was speaking directly to me, saying, "Chernae, it is you I am calling."

17

Jesus. Everyday Good News

EVEN ME - PART 2

Chernae Saka

Over and over, God had made it abundantly clear to me that the messages I was hearing were specifically crafted for me, and everything He was doing in my life (personally and professionally) was His way of saying, it is you that I am seeking. I remember thinking, how can I deny Him when He has been so good to me? There is no way. The love God showed me broke me down, and in sincere repentance, I said "yes" to His call. *The hymn states, "How could I this Friend deny, when He's so true to me?" (from Jesus is all the world to me by William Lamartine Thompson).* I am a witness that it is truly the goodness of God that leads us to repentance.

Everyday Good News Prayer

Dear Heavenly Father, thank You for Your patience, longsuffering, kindness, mercy, and grace. Thank You for Your gentle dealings with me that call me out of darkness and into Your marvelous light. I receive Your love with my whole heart. I am Yours and You are mine. In Jesus's name, amen!

17

Jesus. Everyday Good News

EVEN ME - PART 2

Chernae Saka

My Reflections on "Even Me - Part 2"

18

Jesus. Everyday Good News

OUR IMPARTIAL GOD

Chernae Saka

...Of a truth I perceive that God is no respecter of persons.
(Acts 10:34, KJV)

In John 4:9, the Samaritan woman said to Jesus, *"How is it that you, a Jew, ask a drink of me, a woman of Samaria? For Jews have no dealings with Samaritans."* This story reminds me that there is nothing really new under the sun. Here, we see that racial, social, religious, and cultural divides existed before and during the time of Jesus. This division was not only the case with the Samaritans but with anyone considered "a Gentile, with the Gentiles being everyone else who was not Jewish.

Yes, God called the Israelites to be His chosen people- caretakers of His promise to the world and a reflection of His character to the nations to help turn their hearts back to the Creator God. Yes, He told them to refrain from mingling, intermarrying, and engaging with other nations to protect them from being turned away from Him and to keep them focused on their mission. Deuteronomy 7:4 explains why: *"For they will turn thy son away from following me, that they may serve other gods."* We can understand that as parents. We train our children to be careful who they hang out with because we don't want them distracted or damaged. Being careful absolutely does not mean their "friends" are not special and we don't care about them. We just know no one is helped if everyone gets off track. What about the Gentiles, what was God's original intent for them?

Notice how God instructed the Israelites to treat those who were not Israelites:

- *Matthew 5:44, Jesus says but I say unto you, love your enemies, bless them that curse you, do good to them that hate you, and pray for them which despitefully use you, and persecute you (KJV).*

18

Jesus. Everyday Good News

OUR IMPARTIAL GOD

Chernae Saka

- *Deuteronomy 10:19, therefore, love the stranger, for you were strangers in the land of Egypt (KJV).*
- *Exodus 23:9 also thou shalt not oppress a stranger: for ye know the heart of a stranger, seeing ye were strangers in the land of Egypt (KJV).*
- *Isaiah 56:6 states that foreigners would be entitled to God's blessings if they would serve and love the name of the Lord (KJV).*

Most likely it was God's hope that such kind treatment would lead foreign nations to Him. This hope was realized in the life of Ruth as she proclaimed that her husband's people would be her people, and her husband's God would be her God (Ruth 1:16). We also see it with Rahab as she was obedient in hiding the spies because she had chosen to believe and trust the God of Israel and His word (Joshua 2:9-12). These two women were blessed in their circumstances and their offspring were counted among the lineage of Jesus Christ (Matthew 1:5). Jesus Christ, in His dealing with mankind, has never shown partiality nor discriminated in His love for the whole world (John 3:16). Every life matters to Him. No one is excluded from His love and blessings.

In Acts 10:9-22, Peter was given a vision of a great sheet descending with all kinds of unclean animals on it. He was instructed to kill and eat. Peter refused saying, *"Lord, I have never eaten anything unclean or common" and then confessed saying, "Ye know how that it is an unlawful then for a man that is a Jew to keep company or come unto one of another nation; but God hath showed me that I should not call any man common or unclean" (Acts 10:28, KJV).*

Thank God, Jesus is not a respecter of persons. He does not favor

18

Jesus. Everyday Good News

OUR IMPARTIAL GOD

Chernae Saka

one person over another or one nation over the other. As Peter said, *"but in every nation he that feareth Him, and worketh righteousness, is accepted with Him* (Acts 10:35, KJV). Jesus Himself said that all who come to Him, He would not cast out or reject (John 6:37).

Everyday Good News Prayer

Dear Heavenly Father, one of humanity's most cherished weaknesses are the racial, social, religious and cultural tensions we use to divide and suppress each other, and to misrepresent the loving Character of God. Have mercy on us God, give us new hearts so that we may cease from feeding all that is not of You. Please tear down these cruel boundaries and territories we have formed and lead us into Your Truth so that we may be one true family of Christ and receive each other as brothers and sisters in Christ, in Jesus' name, Amen.

18

Jesus. Everyday Good News

OUR IMPARTIAL GOD

Chernae Saka

My Reflections on "Our Impartial God"

19

Jesus. Everyday Good News

GOD'S FORGIVENESS-PART 1

Oliver Nelson, III

Him hath God exalted with His right hand to be a Prince and a Savior, for to give repentance to Israel, and forgiveness of sins. (Acts 5:31, KJV)

Every layer of Jesus is pure goodness, and just when we think we've heard it all, God reveals even more good news. Ephesians 1:3-7, Colossians 1:14, and 1 Corinthians 1:30 remind us that in Jesus Christ, we have been given all the spiritual blessings we will ever need: salvation, wisdom, righteousness, sanctification, and the forgiveness of our sins. God was not joking when He said He would supply all our needs based on His riches in glory, as found in Jesus Christ (Philippians 4:19). As soon as Christ chose to become our Savior, He brought to us, in Himself, the full supply of everything we needed: an all-in-One package deal.

Unfortunately, when it comes to forgiveness, we have become confused and think that we must act first before God will forgive us or that we must do something to get Him to forgive us. Act how? Maybe beg hard enough, prove we deserve it, fix ourselves up first, or do enough good works to earn His forgiveness. Thus, what should be good news for every broken sinner becomes a heavy burden, causing painful trauma, misrepresenting the character of God, and leaving helpless sinners like me feeling further damaged, unrepentant, or guilt-ridden.

We are sinners and need to know God's forgiveness no matter where we are in our faith journey. God's forgiveness is a basic human need, not a luxury some can earn, deserve, or afford. Let's be honest. What could you or I, or anyone else, ever do to earn, deserve, or even afford the forgiveness of the God of the universe, the Creator of all things, the Ruler of Heaven and Earth, the Source of all life and power? Absolutely nothing; as such, the only

GOD'S FORGIVENESS-PART 1

Oliver Nelson, III

way for God to get us the forgiveness we need was to freely give it to us in His Son, Jesus Christ. In looking at God's forgiveness from texts like Isaiah 43:25, 53:6; Colossians 1:14, 2:13; and 1 John 2:12, we notice they are all written in the past tense, indicating that God's forgiveness has already happened. In Christ Jesus, God has already (past tense) forgiven us of all our sins. Wow!

No, this does not mean He is taking sin lightly. God hates sin because of what it is and what it does to those He created and loves. Romans 3:23, 6:23, 3:12, and Isaiah 64:6 remind us that we all have sinned. Sin is coming short of God's glory, not having God's character, going against His lawful character of love, and being devoid of any goodness in ourselves by our nature and actions (1 John 3:4, Isaiah 64:6, Romans 7:18-20). Scripture tells us that sin, if not dealt with, will lead us to eternal death (James 1:15). The only way sin could be conquered was through Jesus paying the penalty for all our sins.

Forgiveness is part of the all-in-one package deal in Christ. Sadly, so many of us spend most of our time begging God for forgiveness rather than thanking God for already having given it to us. Some may think this *"thought"* is too good to be true. Please remember that God promised to supply all our need, and He did so in Christ. God's forgiveness, which only He can provide, is a need of all sinners. We can never earn it, deserve it, or afford it. So rather than me doubting His Word and work, I say, "Amen, praise God, thank You, Jesus. My sins have already been forgiven; that painful load of guilt and shame has been lifted and carried to the cross by my Savior. I have been freed, and whoever the Son sets free, is truly free (John 8:36).

Good News Prayer

Dear Father in Heaven, I am so humbled that You love me so much as to meet all my need in one package, Jesus Christ. Thank you for your forgiveness freely given to me, in Him.

19

Jesus. Everyday Good News

GOD'S FORGIVENESS-PART 1

Oliver Nelson, III

My Reflections on "God's Forgiveness"

20

Jesus. Everyday Good News

GOD'S FORGIVENESS-PART 2

Oliver Nelson, III

If we confess our sins, He is faithful and just to forgive us of our sins and cleanse us of all unrighteousness (1 John 1:9, KJV).

Believe it or not, the good news of God's forgiveness gets even better. Yes, forgiveness means pardon... to give up your right to pay back or release feelings of resentment or revenge toward a person or group who has harmed you, regardless that they do not deserve your forgiveness. Praise God, Jesus Christ did that for us by paying the price for our sins. Unfortunately, what most of us have never paid attention to is that God's forgiveness means even more than just Him legally pardoning us from all our sins. Texts like Isaiah 55:7-9 and Psalms 103:12 show us that forgiveness also involves a separation from sin. Thus, forgiveness means pardoning from all our sins... AND reclaiming, separating, or cleansing us of sin. A famous Christian writer shared that *"God's forgiveness is not merely a judicial act by which He sets us free from condemnation. It is not only forgiveness for sin, but reclaiming from sin..." (Ellen White, Thoughts from the Mount of Blessings, 116).*

We all suffer the pain of guilt over the wrongs we have done and seem to keep doing, as if we are slaves to it. As followers of Jesus Christ, we are so grateful that God has already forgiven us for all our sins, and that act causes us to want more. We want to stop thinking or doing that sin that is harming us and others repeatedly and which of ourselves we are helpless to stop doing. It's frustrating disheartening to keep coming back to God and others saying I'm sorry, I'm sorry, I'm sorry, but having no power to stop our damaging actions, to stop sinning, to change, to separate ourselves from that sin. The love God showed us in freely forgiving us of all our sins changes our hearts; we want more, and we want better, for God, for ourselves, and for others impacted by our actions. We need God to cleanse us (separate us) from our desire for that sin and all sin.

20

Jesus. Everyday Good News

GOD'S FORGIVENESS-PART 2

Oliver Nelson, III

Think about King David. We all know his life story and His need for God's forgiveness. He understood God's forgiveness. He was grateful for it, so much so that he wanted his whole heart cleaned, purged of that desire for wrong. Notice his prayer, *"Create in me a clean heart, O God; and renew a right spirit within me" (Psalms 51:10)*. Later, it seemed like David was rejoicing with relief and hope, for he said, *"As far as the east is from the west, so far hath He removed our transgressions from us (Psalms 103:12, KJV)."* In His great love for us, God gave us what He knew we needed: free forgiveness that equaled pardon and cleansing (separating us from sin).

Why do we rarely hear about the 2 parts of forgiveness? First, Satan doesn't want you ever to know how good God is, and he certainly doesn't want you to be separated from your sins. He's got a hot final event he plans on you joining him in. Another reason is that, in our English Bible, only one word, forgiveness, is used to describe both pardon and cleansing. In the Greek language, in which most of the New Testament was written, charizomai was used to describe pardon, and aphiemi was used to describe God's cleansing or separating from sin. We can see the two parts of forgiveness mentioned in various Bible texts:

- *And you, being dead in your sins and the uncircumcision of your flesh, hath he quickened together with him, having forgiven you all trespasses (Colossians 2:13, KJV).*
- *And when they had nothing to pay, He frankly forgave them both. Tell me therefore, which of them will love him most? (Luke 7:42, KJV),*
- *If we confess our sins, He is faithful and just to forgive us our sins, and to cleanse us from all unrighteousness (1 John 1:9, KJV).*

The forgiveness in Colossians. 2:23 and Luke 7:42 refers to charizomai (pardon), whereas the forgiveness 1 John 1:9 refers to aphiemi (to cleanse or separate from).

GOD'S FORGIVENESS-PART 2

Oliver Nelson, III

The word charizomai comes from the word charis, which means grace. It is the most common meaning, specific to the New Testament, used to mean pardon and graciously forgive a person's sins (The Complete Word Study Dictionary, Spiros Zodhiates Th. D). However, the forgiveness in 1 John 1:9 refers to aphiemi, and it does not mean "pardon." It originates from two root words, "apo" and "hiemi". Apo means "from" and "hiemi" means "send forth" or "send away." Thus, "aphiemi" means sending forth from, separating, or sending away from.

Aphiemi paints a picture of two entities being separated. It is used in Matthew 13:36, *"Then Jesus sent the multitude away, and went into the house,"* the word "sent" is "aphiemi". Also, in 1 Corinthians 7:11, where Paul said, *"Let not the husband put away his wife"*. The words "put away" are also translated from "aphiemi". On a side note, let's thank God for all the deep Bible scholars and students God used and uses to spotlight rich glimpses of His truth for our edification.

From this background, what 1 John 1:9 is telling us is good news. "If we confess our sins, He is faithful and just to" "put away" or "separate us from" our sins and "*cleanse us from all unrighteousness.*' We were already pardoned (CHARIZOMAI) in Christ. Now, our hearts need to be cleansed of the desire for sin (APHIEMI). If we confess (admit to God that we have a problem we cannot overcome and give Him permission to separate us from that sin), He will do so, thus cleansing us from all unrighteousness.

In Christ, God's gift of pardon has been freely given to the whole world (charizomai). This gift is what initiates a desire for cleansing in our hearts. Cleansing is the result of and depends on God's free pardon (charizomai). Cleansing (aphiemi) is God's desired result or fruit of His free pardon of all our sins. God the Creator has a right to forgive (charizomai) whoever He wants to, on whatever terms as He sees fit. It happens to be His character to freely forgive, and He has

20

Jesus. Everyday Good News

GOD'S FORGIVENESS

Oliver Nelson, III

done so. No one can change that truth or take it away from us. However, Jesus cannot force us to let Him separate us from sin. He can only do so with our permission. Thus, God's pardon has been freely given to all, and His cleansing will be experienced by those who consent for Him to do so in their hearts, minds, and lives.

Think about Mary Magdalene in John 8:1-11, John 8:1-11, Luke 7:36-50, and Matthew 18:23-30. We know what she was into, but Mary received God's free gift of pardon, and by her actions, she demonstrated that she wanted cleansing and separation from her sin, and she received it. So much so that Jesus said wherever the gospel would be preached her story and response would be told (Mark 14:9). Sadly, not everyone responds the same as did Mary, as we will see in later devotionals. For now, remember, no one can pay the debt of their sins, which is eternal death, nor can anyone ever earn God's forgiveness. Thus, God has freely forgiven all of us (charizomai), in Jesus Christ. Those of us who choose to believe this powerful gospel truth will obey it by gladly responding to God with gratefulness, and He will lead us to confession and repentance. Then, as He promised, we will experience the removal of sin from our minds, hearts, and lives (aphiemi). I believe, receive, and thank God for His forgiveness -free pardon...and cleansing, how about you?

Good News Prayer

Father in Heaven, what a burden lifted! Now, the focus of my prayers will no longer be please, please forgive me of all my sins; rather, it will be, Father, thank You for loving me so much You have already forgiven me of all my sins, in Jesus Christ. Like Paul, I admit I am the chief of sinners. I give You permission to come into my heart, mind, and life and separate me from that sin that is hurting You, myself, and others; and is misrepresenting Your character to the world. Like David, please cleanse me, create in me a clean heart, and give me back Your right spirit so that my life can honor You. In Jesus name, amen.

20

Jesus. Everyday Good News

GOD'S FORGIVENESS-PART 2

Oliver Nelson, III

My Reflections on "God's Forgiveness-Part 2"

21

Jesus. Everyday Good News

THAT ONE CHOICE

Sharon PergersonI

For as in Adam all die, even so in Christ all shall be made alive.
(1 Corinthians 15:22, KJV)

Imagine Adam waking up on that late Friday afternoon of creation with his Creator standing over him with a smile that radiated pure love and joy. Adam probably gazed in wonderment at the beautiful, perfect world created for him as he explored all the intricacies of creation. Then, he noticed there was no companion for him as for God's other creations, and after falling asleep, he awoke to a beautiful woman beside him, his own helpmate or companion. God had indeed supplied his every need. We wished the story would go on in sweet innocence, but a few chapters later, Adam made that one choice that changed the course of his life and the life of the whole human family, inflicting sin and death upon all.

That one choice of distrusting God, disbelieving His Word, and loving something and someone more than he loved His Creator led him to disobey God's warning not to eat from the fruit of the tree of the knowledge of good and evil. God never wanted Adam to come to know the pain and torture of knowing good and evil. Now, Adam would have to live with the knowledge that he would die because of that one choice. Now, every moment of joy he experienced was attached to pain, fear, guilt, and sorrow, which he could not escape from.

His new "reality" must have woken him up in the morning and was the last thing he thought about at night. During the day, he may have hidden himself in the bushes as he felt the results of that one choice on his relationship with God, himself, his family, and the world his Creator had made for him. His heart was probably close to exploding as he saw the havoc that ensued- family discord, the murder of one son by another son, and some of his children making

21

Jesus. Everyday Good News

THAT ONE CHOICE

Sharon Pergerson

choices to reject God. I believe he grieved watching the animals he loved become fearful of him, distant, and aggressive. As he toiled on the land, how frustrating it must have been that it no longer produced what it could have, nor was as easy as it had been before, as if it was fighting Him.

The only thing strong enough to hold him together was the promise that his Creator had made to the serpent, Satan, who had robbed them of their perfect relationship with God, with themselves, with others, and with all that He created for them (see Genesis 3:15, KJV). I believe when the Creator covered Adam and Eve with the skin of a sacrificed lamb, Adam better understood that his Creator would someday give his life to save them from that one bad choice. Adam's son, Abel, continued that act of sacrifice, demonstrating his belief and acceptance in a coming Savior, while Cain rejected it. Every time Eve had a child, she likely hoped that child was their promised Savior (see Genesis 4:1-4).

We know the rest of the story, and it would be a very sad story if it began and ended at this point. However, even before Adam's one wrong choice, Jesus Christ, the Creator, had already made one right choice that impacted Adam and everyone in his lineage. It was the initiating actions of Jesus that made Adam's hope a promised reality. That one choice, made by God the Father, the Son, and the Holy Spirit, ensured that if ever the human family chose to sin, there was a Savior in place to save them from sin. Revelation 13:8 tells us that Jesus was the Lamb slain from the foundation of the world. Long before Adam and you and I were created and decided to sin, Jesus had already committed to giving his life for, or in place of, the one we destroyed. This wasn't an afterthought. This was a plan thought of in the heart of the Father, the Son, and the Holy Spirit before They even created the world.

21

Jesus. Everyday Good News

THAT ONE CHOICE

Sharon Pergerson

Think about it, there was already a Savior as soon as there was sin. Likewise, Jesus already had a solution in place before you made that one bad choice that you cannot fix: His life for yours. Jesus, through His birth, life, death, and resurrection, paid the ultimate consequence of eternal death for all your sins and mine. That one choice, that one decision of Jesus, changed the trajectory of your destiny and mine. You may be somewhere in the dark, hurting over a decision that has ruined your life or eradicated your opportunity to make other decisions you would have loved to make. Every day, you're reminded of that one bad decision. Maybe it wakes you up in the morning, causes you restless nights, and has driven you to more damaging behaviors. Every moment of joy you experience has attached to it pain, fear, guilt, and sorrow, from which you cannot escape.

Paul understood it. He felt the war of sin raging in his body; with every good he did, he could still feel the presence of evil within him, in his members, like a terminal disease raging through his body. No wonder He cried out in Romans 7:24, *"Oh wretched man that I am who shall deliver me from the body of this death."* Then, in verse 25, he answered his question and thanked God that through Jesus Christ our Lord, he had a way of escape, a means of deliverance.

Dear child of God and co-believer in Jesus Christ, sin hurts-it kills, steals, and destroys, but do not despair or give up hope. Ours is not a lost cause. Jesus's right choice has been given to us as a gift, and His perfect sinless life and his death on the cross, paid the price for all our wrong choices. Now, because of Jesus, all that Satan has killed, stolen, or destroyed in our lives will be one day restored. Now, because of Jesus, one day soon and very soon, we will know and experience only good, without any evil attached.

21

Jesus. Everyday Good News

THAT ONE CHOICE

Sharon Pergerson

Take courage in God has done for us in Christ, including the future He willed for us, promised us, and died to ensure for us. Let's live in it right now, from this day forward, keeping in mind 1 John 5:11-13:

"This is the record that God has given to us eternal life, and this life is in His Son. He that hath the Son hath life; And he that hath not the Son of God hath not life. These things I have written unto you that believe on the name of the Son of God; That ye may know that ye have eternal life and that ye may believe on the name of the Son of God" (KJV).

This is God's official promise to every sinner, to every human being who has made wrong moves, wrong decisions, and that one wrong choice. That's real good news at an eternal level, praise God.

Good News Prayer

Dear Father in Heaven, I have messed up so badly, and I can't fix it. Thank you for being the Savior of those who are lost, helpless, broken, and feel forsaken. I am so grateful for Your forgiveness, of not only that wrong choice that's the elephant in my life, but of all my sins. Like the thief on the cross, I have one choice left that matters eternally. I am making that choice today. I choose to believe and receive what You have done for me in Jesus Christ, my Creator, Savior, and Lord. No matter what I am about to face in this temporal life, I know You are and will remain with me. I accept the future You have gifted to me, and I renounce the life sin has used to imprison me. I rest in Your promise to me and thank You for it. In Jesus's name, I pray, amen.

21

Jesus. Everyday Good News

THAT ONE CHOICE

Sharon Pergerson

My Reflections on "That One Choice"

SECTION TWO

As broken people we all need everyday good news about what Jesus can and will do in our everyday lives.

22

Jesus. Everyday Good News

BE YE HOLY

Chernae Saka

...Because it is written, Be ye Holy; for I am Holy. (1 Peter 1:16, KJV)

In life's journey, we often encounter the pressure to strive for greatness, set goals, have ambitions, and relentlessly pursue perfection. After a while, this mindset can become draining, tiresome, and even discouraging, leading some to contemplate quitting altogether. The Apostle Paul, in Romans 7:15-24, candidly expresses his struggle between his aspirations and his present reality, a struggle familiar to many.

What is God truly calling us to? Is it to chase unrelenting ambition and perfection? According to 1 Peter 1:16, we are called to be holy because God is holy. He is essentially calling us to be like Him. In verse 15, Peter emphasizes that the One who called us is holy, is urging us to be holy in all aspects of life. The Greek word *anastrohe*, translated as *conversation* in verse 15, encompasses all life, conduct, behavior, and deportment. Holiness is presented not as a mere pursuit of a thing but as a state of being—a lifestyle and a higher standard of living that is a reflection of the life of Jesus.

1 Peter 1:18-19 underscores the cost of our salvation; it was paid not with perishable gold or silver but with the precious blood of Christ, the sinless, spotless Lamb of God. This lavish act demands a response from each of us, a choice to either ignore what was done for us or submit to God's calling. Peter, recognizing this, encourages us to prepare our minds for action and self-control in verse 13, cautioning against slipping back into our old ways. As we all know that's easier said than done. Too many of us try and assume the responsibility of holiness upon ourselves, and we fail every time. It's a weight we have no strength to bear, believe me, I am a witness. How, then, are we to become holy?

BE YE HOLY

Chernae Saka

It's crucial not to automatically assume the responsibility of holiness on ourselves. To be holy, we must step back, believe, grasp the promises of God by faith, and allow Him to work His will in us. So, while God has called all of us to the high calling of being holy (Leviticus 20:7), notice how we, helpless sinners, are to achieve this by reading 1 Corinthians 1: 2, 30; 2 Corinthians 5:21, and Ephesians 6:26.

All the beautiful Bible promises we read affirm to us that it is God who works in us to make us holy (Lev. 20:8); we don't have to and cannot make ourselves holy. The process of God making us holy, also called sanctification, involves setting us apart for a holy purpose, only He can do that. We yield our will to Him, and He does the work of making us holy. What a weight lifted, and victory guaranteed. Thank You, Jesus.

Everyday Good News Prayer:

Dear Heavenly Father, help us comprehend Your marvelous plan to make us holy, as You are holy. As Your Holy Spirit instructs and corrects us, may we not neglect or push You away. You have called us to be holy, a most beautiful reflection of your character to the world, and this is Your intent for each of us. May we yield to Your transformative work. In Jesus's name, Amen.

22

Jesus. Everyday Good News

BE YE HOLY

Chernae Saka

My Reflections on "Be Ye Holy"

23

Jesus. Everyday Good News

NO PART WITH ME

Chernae Saka

"Peter said to Him, "You shall never wash my feet!" Jesus answered him, "If I do not wash you, you have no part with Me." (John 13:8, NKJV)

Recently a thought came to me that hit me hard. It was tough to swallow, but so healing and freeing to me, and I hope it will be the same for you. Oftentimes we exalt our political affiliations, professional accomplishments, nationality, culture, and even gender. We see these characteristics as worthy of defining our identity. Exodus 20:3 says, *"You shall have no other gods before Me."* Is it possible that as followers of Christ, we are violating this command by exalting our characteristics above our identity in Christ?

I thought about Paul. Paul had it all. He was the cream of the crop. If anyone could boast about what gave them their worth or identity (according to human standards), it was Paul. Yet, when he yielded his heart to Jesus Christ, he said he counted all his professional accomplishments and culture as a loss, just so that he might win Christ (Philippians 3:4-8). To me, this meant that Paul allowed himself to be cleansed of any and everything, or ideology that exalted itself above God or God's Word in his life. He considered it all as dung or rubbish, so that He could gain Jesus Christ as Lord of His life. He gave it all up, let it go, in exchange for Christ.

The work of God in our lives, often termed sanctification, is a process that occurs throughout our lifetime. The biblical definition of sanctification is "to set apart for special use of purpose," that is, to make holy or sacred. Jesus calls those who follow Him, His people, His body, or His church. Ephesians 5:25-26 illustrates God's intent for His people by explaining that Christ so loved the church, that He gave his life for it. Jesus didn't just stop with giving His life. He gave his life so that He could set us apart and cleanse us. We see that in

23

Jesus. Everyday Good News

NO PART WITH ME

Chernae Saka

2 Corinthians 5:21, *God made Jesus sin for us, so that we may be made the righteousness of God in Christ Jesus.* It has always been God's intent to save us from the penalty, power, and presence of sin.

On the night of the Passover, Jesus demonstrated what He was going to do in the life of the believer. John 13:4 indicates that Jesus laid aside his garments, took a towel, and girded himself. This very act is paralleled in Philippians 2:7, "but made Himself of no reputation, taking the form of a bondservant, and coming in the likeness of men." Peter protested this act, perhaps he thought, "How could my Rabbi do such a demeaning thing?" These acts are usually performed by the servants of the household. Jesus' response was, "if I don't wash you, you have no part with Me." What is Jesus saying? Simply, if we do not allow God to sanctify us or cleanse us from sin, we cannot say we have a part with Him.

We cannot say that I am a European Christian, a Republican Christian, an American Christian, a Gay Christian, or even a Liberal Christian, because anything we place before us being a believer in Christ can become idolatrous to us. The sanctification process not only includes Jesus washing and cleansing us of our sins, but also setting things in their proper place. Paul said it best in 2 Corinthians 5:17, "*Therefore if any man be in Christ, he is a new creature; old things are passed away; behold, all things have become new.*" *(KJV)*

Every Day Good News

Dear Heavenly Father, it is our prayer that we exalt nothing before You and that we allow Jesus to sanctify us day by day. In Jesus' name, Amen.

23

Jesus. Everyday Good News

NO PART WITH ME

Chernae Saka

My Reflections on "No Part of Me"

24

Jesus. Everyday Good News

LESSONS FROM THE GRASS

Sharon Pergerson

For all flesh is as grass. And all the glory of man as the flower of grass. The grass withereth, and the flower thereof falleth away: but the word of the Lord endureth for ever. (1 Peter 1:24-25, KJV)

Imagine luscious, green grass everywhere, a long-awaited sight after many harsh winters and wet springs. I enjoy walking barefoot through warm grass and lying on its soft spikes. Most of us never think much about grass; we know it turns brown as winter nears and it turns green in the Spring in some parts of the world. We take for granted its commonness and are irritated at its rapid growth. From our actions, it seems like we have come to think that grass grows by itself, and that God has nothing to do with insignificant strings of grass, which today is alive, and tomorrow is cut down and thrown away.

We often think of God as so far away and busy that He has no time to look after the small details of His world. We forget that looking after and caring for all His creations and creatures, from the greatest to the least, is His special work. Part of what makes God so great is His ability to handle the greatest feats, like keeping the stars and planets in place, yet still paying close attention to the tiniest details, like growing grass.

We rarely wonder at the appearance of grass, yet we should. There is a wonder about even grass. Remember when the Word of God said, "*Let the earth bring forth grass*" (Genesis 1:11)? From then till now, His Word is still causing the earth to bring forth grass. Have you ever noticed a tiny blade of grass or corn push its way up to the surface despite heavy dirt clods? Have you ever seen a tiny sprout so tender it cannot support its weight, barely has color, and is made up of mostly water? If you crushed it, only moisture would be left on

LESSONS FROM THE GRASS

Sharon Pergerson

your hand. Yet this same tiny thing, a blade of grass, can push up through dirt ten thousand times its weight. Where does grass get that kind of power from, itself? Try it and see. Cut a full-grown blade of grass, cover it with a small amount of dirt, and see what will happen: nothing. Now, take a paper-thin blade and see if it will stand upright in your hand. It can't, nor is there scarcely anything weaker. Yet, just a few minutes before, it was standing tall. Talk about a miracle? What is the power seen in the grass? It's the power of God's Word. There is no power in the grass itself, but that feeble instrument displays the mighty power of God's Word to every human being.

Really, what's the big deal about God causing the grass to grow anyway? It is a reminder that helps us recognize God's power in small things. Since God takes the time to make grass grow, surely, He will do for us what we need. We are as weak as grass; we have no power in and of ourselves, although we would like to think so. *"All flesh is grass"* (Isaiah 40:6). Any life we have, any power we have access to is from God. That's both a very humbling and uplifting thought. I am like a blade of grass, but God cares so tenderly for me and gives me His life and power to push through life's many deep, dark hurdles. So, although I have no power in myself, I can still "*do all things through Christ, who strengthens me.*" (Philippians 4:13).

Now we can better understand Paul's response to the Words of God in 2 Corinthians 12:9-10:

> *"And He (God) said unto me, My grace is sufficient for thee: for My strength is made perfect in weakness. Most gladly therefore will I (Paul) rather glory in my infirmities (weaknesses), that the power of Christ may*

LESSONS FROM THE GRASS

Sharon Pergerson

rest upon me. Therefore, I take pleasure in infirmities, in reproaches, in necessities, in persecutions, in distresses for Christ's sake: for when I am weak, then am I strong." (KJV)

Let's take courage, my brother and sister. Like dirt, life weighs heavily upon all of us; unfortunately, that probably won't change this side of heaven. But today and every day, we are so blessed to have a God who specializes in making the impossible possible, making a way out of no way, and doing for us that which we cannot do for ourselves.

Some may be upset that God compares you and me to weak grass, but don't be. Let's thank Him for using our weakness to display His power and strength. Our weakness is a fact, but it is not a disability if we let God's strength work in us. I believe God wants me and you to get this point deep into our minds and hearts; maybe that's why He created so much luscious green grass everywhere. So, when I do get to walk through the grass again, I'll enjoy it even more, for it is a reminder that the same Word of God that causes the grass to break through the dirt is powerful enough to bring me and you, up and through whatever weight, problem, or situation we face in life.

Everyday Good News Prayer

Dear Father in Heaven, I admit and submit to the fact that I am as weak as grass and can do nothing without You. Thank You for being willing to display Your power upon me and for doing for me that which I cannot do for myself, I receive it by faith today and every day. In Jesus name, amen.

24

Jesus. Everyday Good News

LESSONS FROM THE GRASS

Sharon Pergerson

My Reflections on "Lessons from the Grass"

25

Jesus. Everyday Good News

FORGIVING ONE ANOTHER

Oliver Nelson, III

And be kind to one another, tenderhearted, forgiving one another, even as God in Christ forgave you. (Ephesians 4:32, KJV)

Forgiving others hits a tender spot in us all. To be honest, it is unnatural for us to forgive those who have wronged us. Indeed, even when we possess the best intentions, we often find the motivation to forgive lacking. However, the above Bible verse describes a profoundly different reason we should forgive those who have wronged us: God in Christ has forgiven us for the wrongs we have committed against Him.

Let's consider the experience of Jesus for a bit. While Jesus hung on that cross, bludgeoned, bleeding, and being tormented by the very beings He created and came to save, the Bible records that He offered a prayer of forgiveness for His tormentors: *"Father forgive them for they know not what they do"* (Luke 23:34). I believe that prayer of forgiveness was not just for them, but for the whole world, including me and you. What is all the more astounding, yet sobering is that Christ was not suffering for Himself on that cross – He was suffering for you and me, the just for the unjust (1 Peter 3:18). He was "wounded for our transgressions;" He was *"bruised for our iniquities,"* even though He had not committed one act of sin (See Isaiah 53:5-6).

The weight of all of our sins crushed out the life of the Son of God on the cross. If anyone had a reason not to forgive, it was Christ. No matter the extent to which you and I have been wronged, no one in the history of the human race has been treated more unjustly than Jesus. He was the most wronged. Yet God's heart was too full of love and compassion for His wayward children not to allow Him to forgive us. He forgave without provocation and without expecting anything in response to His forgiving spirit. Simply put, Christ forgave us because His love for us compelled Him to do so. Jesus has forgiven you and me for the worst trespasses we have committed against Him, for His Name's sake. Thus, it would seem like we should be willing to forgive those who have wronged us easily.

Jesus understands that of ourselves, we can do nothing; we are too weak and too damaged, and sometimes we can't "just" forgive. Some things are too traumatizing just to erase from our lives, as it were. Sin hurts; it steals, kills, and destroys (John 10:10). So, Jesus doesn't just say go forgive on your own, Oliver. He does so much more. As I yield to Him being the Lord of my life, He takes control. He brings His gift of His forgiveness into my heart (Acts 5:31). Then, because you and I are so weak and wounded, with our permission, He does the forgiving in and through us to those who have wronged us deeply. How is that? Because God promised to supply our need, and to do the work of His will in us and through us; in every area of our lives and His promises never fail (Philippians 2:13).

In the parable of the unforgiving servant in Matthew 18: 21-35, that servant was forgiven by the kind king of a huge amount he could never repay, forgiveness He did not even ask for; yet he was about to destroy a fellow servant because that servant owed him a tiny sum of money. What was that about? I believe the real issue was that the unforgiving servant did not realize the enormity of his debt and the impossibility of paying it back, and he did not value the priceless gift of forgiveness (pardon) given to him. Maybe this was because he did not value the king and his grace, nor did he want to reflect the character of the king to others. That may be why the king called him a wicked servant. What about us? Do we value the gift of forgiveness

25

Jesus. Everyday Good News

FORGIVING ONE ANOTHER

Oliver Nelson, III

God has freely given to all of us in Jesus Christ, at the cost of His life, and so much so that we are willing to yield and allow His forgiveness to flow from Him to us to others, regardless of their wrongs against us. Do we value our King Jesus enough to let Him work in us and through us to reflect His character of forgiveness to others?

Everyday Good News Prayer

Lord, Thank You for Your divine forgiveness. You are Lord of all things, including vengeance, yet You have never shown me the contempt I deserve for the sins I've committed against you and yours. Thank You for Your grace that paid the penalty of all sin, and for Your love that moves me to repentance! I receive your forgiveness and yield to You sharing it through me to others so they may experience the kindness of Your forgiving character and be led to open their hearts to You. Amen and amen.

25

Jesus. Everyday Good News

FORGIVING ONE ANOTHER

Oliver Nelson, III

My Reflections on "Forgiving One Another"

26

Jesus. Everyday Good News

THE SPIRIT OF NATHAN

Sharon Pergerson

And Nathan said to David, Thou art the Man... (2 Samuel 12:7, KJV)

In the story of Nathan and King David in 2 Samuel 12, David had Uriah the Hittite, one of his best soldiers, killed because he had impregnated Uriah's wife, Bathsheba, and he wanted to marry her. Who would dare say anything to him? He could do what he wanted as king, or so he may have thought. I am sure David tried to return to being a "good leader" after that. When God sent Nathan the prophet, to him with a story of one man coveting and stealing another man's prized possession, David gave the right verdict: it was wrong, so wrong, and that man deserved death. Then Nathan told David he was that man who cruelly wronged another man, in his actions towards Uriah and Bathsheba. Nathan shared that after all God had blessed him with, David was in a position where God had given him everything he needed and so much of whatever he wanted.

As I thought about it, I wondered why God had Nathan confront David. It may be that God had to deal with David's actions because of who He was as God, who David was as His son and the leader of His people, and because of the message David's actions sent to the "enemies" or haters of God. From David's response to the confrontation, he seemed somewhat relieved at being "outed," for he said, *"I have sinned against God."* This was about a year after his cruel actions, because the resulting baby was one year old. Notice something: Nathan had told David that God had already forgiven him, so he would not die, although there would be grave consequences for his actions. God had forgiven David before Nathan "outed" him and before he had even confessed. Wow. Again, why then was Nathan sent to Him and why the need for admission, confession, and repentance?

26

Jesus. Everyday Good News

THE SPIRIT OF NATHAN

Sharon Pergerson

I believe Romans 2:4 gives us a clue, *"Or despisest thou the riches of His goodness and forbearance and longsuffering; not knowing that the goodness of God leadeth thee to repentance (KJV)?* David was closer to God than most of us. He knew the richness of God's goodness, forbearance, and longsuffering. At this dark time of his life, he had messed up badly; he knew he had hurt God and probably couldn't even face Him. Most likely, David's pride was crushed. He was embarrassed at his actions, which misrepresented God. Although everyone already knew, he may have been worried about what people would think and do if he admitted his wrongdoing. Guilt was undoubtedly eating him up. All the relationships that He was steward over were damaged: his relationship with God, with himself, with others, and with his responsibilities.

David had humiliated and shamed the One he was known to love and serve; that had to be rough. God already knew that David was imprisoned by sin and its fruit, pride, guilt, shame, and remorse. He knew that David could never be who He designed and called him to be, in this space. The Holy Spirit who spoke through Nathan was sent to set David free, not to destroy Him, but rather to restore Him and to begin the process of rebuilding His damaged relationships. For God to be allowed to replace his faulty heart, David was first reminded of His condition as a sinner. To build him up, David was reminded of God's free forgiveness to him and its implications; he would not die from his sins, and he would not be lost forever because God had already found a way to pay for his sins.

The good news for us every day is that the words Nathan said to David, *"Thou art the man,"* are for me and you. We are the sinners. We have all wronged others, though maybe we haven't done the same as David, or maybe we have done worse. No matter what we have done, God has already forgiven us all our sins by laying them on Jesus Christ (Isaiah 53:4-6). Thus, when God sends the Spirit of Nathan, His Holy Spirit, to us, it isn't to humiliate and destroy us; it is so that He can point out our faulty, wicked hearts so we won't trust in them and so we can see how much we need a Savior. Then He builds us by reminding us of God's free forgiveness to us and what that means; we will not die from our sins forever because Christ has paid the penalty for all of them. That sweet goodness of God will lead the followers of Christ to be the first to confess, repent, restore, and become ministers of reconciliation (2 Corinthians 5:18). As such, whenever we hear that voice, the voice of the Holy Spirit, no matter how painfully true His word is to us, we need not harden our hearts for He comes with the good news we need to be healed, restored, and to move forward and upward.

Everyday Good News Prayer

Dear Father in Heaven, I am "the man." I have wronged and damaged so many others with my selfishness and self-centeredness. God, You have sent the Spirit of Nathan to me many times and I brushed Him off because I didn't want to admit and face my wrongdoing. I had no idea that He came to point out my sin to start the process of setting me free from all the guilt and shame my actions have inflicted upon me. He also came to begin healing and restoring my broken relationships. While I have been perplexed on how to get You to forgive me, and You've already done so. You've forgiven me of all my sins. Praise God, I confess, I repent, and by Your grace, help me do whatever You need me to do to collaborate with You in Your ministry of reconciliation.

26

Jesus. Everyday Good News

THE SPIRIT OF NATHAN

Sharon Pergerson

My Reflections on "The Spirit of Nathan"

27

Jesus. Everyday Good News

THE RIGHT RESPONSE

Sharon Pergerson

And the King shall answer and say unto them, verily I say unto you, since you have done it unto one of the least of these my brethren, you have done it unto Me. Matthew 25:40 (KJV)

When we hear about forgiveness, it is often spoken to the one wronged, almost drowning them with the truth that as followers of Christ, we must freely forgive those who have wronged us, as He has freely forgiven us. To be honest, forgiveness is not as hard when one looks at all Christ has done for us and all He has forgiven us of.

One problem that forgivers face is that while they forgive those who wronged them, it doesn't automatically make things right between them and those who have wronged them. Reconciliation does not automatically happen because one party forgives. Why is that so? Maybe it's because we most often only look at half the picture. Let's look deeper at the whole picture.

I believe God's forgiveness is not the end-destination of God's intent; rather, it is the beginning of the process. Our response of forgiveness toward others is the right response to God's free forgiveness of us, but it is also not the end destination (Ephesians 4:18). We don't often talk about it, but forgiveness, in and of itself, is not the whole picture, though it should be. God's free forgiveness should cause us to respond with confession and repentance towards God, it should cause us to grant free forgiveness to those who've wronged us, and it should lead those who have wronged us and others to confession and repentance towards God and toward those they have wronged.

Unfortunately, things don't usually work like that. Although God has forgiven all humanity of their sins, He knows that that is not enough to get all humanity into eternal life, nor is it enough to

THE RIGHT RESPONSE

Sharon Pergerson

reconcile the relationship between humanity and Himself because of one thing... our choice and the hardness of our hearts. For things to work as God has planned, there must be a positive, right response to God's forgiveness, a change of heart and mind towards God and His way. That can only result from the choice of all parties to submit to the voice of the Holy Spirit. Only then can there be any chance of reconciliation, which is the restoration of a friendly relationship between all parties. That is what God aims for; *reconciliation has always been God's goal* (2 Corinthians 5:18-20).

Why is reconciliation so important to God? Because we are all one family, His family. How we treat one another, even those we consider the least, the nobodies, the ones we would never humble ourselves to apologize to, is how we treat our family, God's family; with Christ being the head (1 Corinthians 12:12-27). In addition, because Christ has connected Himself with His human family, He identifies Himself as us; His life gives us each life (Colossians 3:4). We are all His children, a part of Him (Galatians 3:26, Ephesians 1:5). Wronging one another wrongs Him (Matthew 25:40-45). Parents and children who love each other can understand this, and we've heard it before: *"You mess with my family, you mess with me."*

The good news is that God has freely forgiven us no matter what we have done to one another and to Him. Infact it is His goodness that even leads us to repent in the first place (Romans 2:4). Our rightful response to such lavish kindness will yield a desire for repentance, confession, and reconciliation with God and those we have wronged. We have all been in the seat as both the victim and the perpetrator of wrong, hurt, and harm. Thankfully, Jesus's everyday good news still extends its long arms to reach both sides of us.

27

Jesus. Everyday Good News

THE RIGHT RESPONSE

Sharon Pergerson

As we receive His free forgiveness into our hearts, it will lead us to be the first to forgive those who have wronged us, freely, and the first to confess and repent when we have wronged others. Then, those humbling, healing words that we too often resist saying will flow freely and sincerely from one member of God's family to another, "*I have wronged God and you, and I am so sorry; I have asked God to cleanse me of this insane desire to wrong His children who are my family, and I am asking for your forgiveness and prayer for me in my journey of cleansing. While I can never undo my wrong towards you, my prayer is that God help me find a way to lessen the pain I caused you.*" What a powerful response toward God there would be if His followers would lead the way in demonstrating to one another, and to the world, the right response of all parties to God's free gift of forgiveness.

Everyday Good News Prayer

Lord, this was another painful read; however, I received it in Jesus' name, amen.

"Therefore, if any man is in Christ, he is a new creature: all things are passed away; behold, all things become new. And all things are of God, who hath reconciled us to himself by Christ Jesus, and have given us the ministry of reconciliation; to wit that God was in Christ, reconciling the world unto Himself, not imputing their trespasses unto them; and have committed unto us the word of reconciliation. Now then, we are ambassadors for Christ, as though God did beseech you by us: we pray you in Christ's stead and be reconciled to God. For He hath made Him sin for us, who knew no sin; That we might be made the righteousness of God in Him.
2 Corinthians 5:17- 21 (KJV).

27

Jesus. Everyday Good News

THE RIGHT RESPONSE

Sharon Pergerson

My Reflections on "The Right Response"

28

Jesus. Everyday Good News

LET THIS MIND BE IN YOU

Oliver Nelson, III

Let this mind be in you, which was also in Christ Jesus.
(Philippians 2:5, KJV)

In the above text, the Apostle Paul appears to be bidding us to receive the mindset of Christ. Christ's mindset was one of humility and obedience, even to the point of death on the cross. Naturally, as humans, we possess a "carnal mind," a mindset that is at enmity with God and is not subject to the law of God, nor can it be (Romans 8:7). A carnal mind is a mindset controlled by the flesh, which will not allow us to live a life that pleases God (Romans 8:8).

From my studies and life experience, I have learned that the flesh is a self-destructive force within us that is determined to satisfy the cravings of our sinful nature. The lust of the flesh (the craving to satisfy our physical and sexual appetite), the lust of the eyes (the craving to satisfy what our eyes see), and the pride of life (the craving to satisfy our selfish ambition) are the three key elements that compose the flesh (1 John 2:16). The Bible describes that living a life *in the flesh* is living only to please one's selfish desires and will result in eternal death (Romans 8:6). Jesus once said that it is the Spirit that giveth life, but the flesh profiteth nothing (John 6:63). Paul once declared that within his flesh dwelled nothing good (Romans 7:18).

In contrast, the mind of Christ is one that is completely emptied of self. In describing the mindset of Christ, Paul says that Christ made Himself of no reputation, which in the original Greek means that Christ emptied himself of his self (Philippians 2:6-7). When Jesus walked this earth, he did not possess to a mindset that compelled him to selfishly satisfy or serve Himself, rather, He possessed and maintained a mindset that compelled Him to unselfishly serve others and perform the will of His Father.

28

Jesus. Everyday Good News

LET THIS MIND BE IN YOU

Oliver Nelson, III

The ultimate will of God the Father was for Christ to serve humanity by dying for humanity on the cross. Jesus was obedient to that, even to the point of death on the cross. Jesus's self-surrendered, self-denying mindset led Him to the cross, and because of his self-denial, God the Father exalted His name above all others. The mindset of Christ is so unlike ours, yet this is the only mindset we can possess that will allow us to live lives pleasing to God.

The bad news is that we cannot have this self-emptying mindset by following Christ's example, acting it out, or practicing it profusely. Notice that the command, "*Let this mind*(set) *be in you*," is written in the passive voice, indicating that the subject receives the action rather than performing it of themselves. I believe this suggests that Paul is urging us to be open and receptive to God working in us to give us a new mindset, attitude, and perspective on life, that aligns with that of Christ Jesus. The same frame of mind and approach to earthly life that Christ embodied is what God seeks to cultivate within us. He will successfully do it if we "let" Him. That is my desire, what about you?

Everyday Good News Prayer

Dear Father, Thank You for showing me what true humility looks like in Jesus Christ, my righteousness. I know that anything I try to do of myself is tainted by sin. I give You permission to "let" Your mind(set) be in me so that I might rightfully reflect Your character to others. In Jesus's name I pray, amen.

28

Jesus. Everyday Good News

LET THIS MIND BE IN YOU

Oliver Nelson, III

My Reflections on "Let this Mind be in You"

29

Jesus. Everyday Good News

WHAT'S MOST VALUABLE

Chernae Saka

But what things were gain to me, those I counted loss for Christ. Yea doubtless, and I count all things but loss for the excellency of the knowledge of Christ Jesus my Lord: for whom I have suffered the loss of all things, and do count them but dung, that I may win Christ, and be found in him, not having mine own righteousness, which is of the law, but that which is through the faith of Christ, the righteousness which is of God by faith. (Philippians 3:7-9, KJV)

We would all agree that a decorated Military Vet, an FBI negotiator, an honorable teacher, an ER Physician, an Engineer, an IT Executive Manager, a University Provost, and a Celebrity Chef are individuals who have received numerous years of education, training, and experience. We would also consider these individuals role models with careers to ascribe to. In Philippians 3:4-6, Paul gives a glimpse of his curriculum vitae (CV) or resume. However, when God captured and transformed Paul's life, the effect was so profound that he found no need to cling to his list of achievements. In fact, the very things he considered assets (something to improve his standing in society) a loss for the sake of Christ. What a change in perspective. This is not to say we should not pursue an education or a better career because nothing is wasted when we allow Christ into our lives.

However, Paul is saying his value system has changed. He emphasizes that the most important thing is knowing Jesus Christ. He further says in verse 9, *"and being found in Him not having my righteousness."* When Paul's conversion took place in Acts 9, one thing became clear: Paul was stripped of his sight and self-importance. Upon regaining his sight, he realized that if this is the walk he was being called to, it could not be done in his own strength. It could not be a mindset of, *"Lord, I will walk with You, however I will do things my way."*

29

Jesus. Everyday Good News

WHAT'S MOST VALUABLE

Chernae Saka

Paul discarded his self-righteousness and clung wholeheartedly to the righteousness of Christ, which is by faith. Paul had a singular eye and a singular focus on Christ. He said, *"I am determined to know nothing among you save Christ, and Him crucified" (1 Corinthians 2:2).* Despite all the education, training, and experience he had received throughout the years, he found (by God's Grace) what was most valuable. Like Paul, may God always keep before us what is truly most valuable.

Everyday Good News Prayer

Heavenly Father, we thank You for the opportunities You have afforded us. May we, like Paul, be brought to the same conclusion that all of our gains have their place, but what is most valuable is that we know who You are, and we know You, personally. May we also be found in Christ, not having our own righteousness, but the righteousness found only through faith in Jesus Christ. We thank you, Lord, Amen,

29

Jesus. Everyday Good News

WHAT'S MOST VALUABLE

Chernae Saka

My Reflections on "What's Most Valuable"

30

Jesus. Everyday Good News

THE ULTIMATE COMPARISON

Chernae Saka

Then said I, Woe is me! for I am undone; because I am a man of unclean lips, and I dwell in the midst of a people of unclean lips: for mine eyes have seen the King, the LORD of hosts. (Isaiah 6:5, KJV)

One Fall morning, I sat in church listening to the elder's offertory response. It was meant to be a call to action for the members to give more in tithe and to the local budget because the church was in deficit. He stated, "As you know, we are unlike other denominations where all the tithe stays at the church. Our pastors do not get directly paid from the members, and they are not driving around in fancy cars like other pastors." It seemed like the elder's offertory response was steeped in the comparison of "us" versus "them." This kind of thinking can be very dangerous because it is so easy to adopt an ultra-superior complex.

Interestingly, Jesus's mind worked in quite the opposite way. Philippians 3:8 reminds us that Christ humbled himself and became obedient unto death, even the death of the cross. Do you ever find yourself saying, *"Well, at least I am not as bad as so and so?"* or *"At least I don't do this or that like so and so?"* Oftentimes, we compare ourselves with fellow human beings, and when we do so, we will always find something about us worth elevating over the next person. However, if we were to adjust who we compare ourselves to, our elevation would immediately lead to humiliation.

Isaiah calls out six 'woes' in Isaiah 5. These woes are words of threatening, lamenting, and admonishing. These woes are directed towards God's chosen people. However, when we get to Isaiah 6:5, the woe that Isaiah expresses is a passionate cry of grief or despair. Notice that Isaiah spoke no words. He saw the Lord high and lifted.

30

Jesus. Everyday Good News

THE ULTIMATE COMPARISON

Chernae Saka

He saw the train of His robe. He saw the angels crying, "Holy, Holy, Holy." He saw the power of God in all His glory and majesty. Through that seeing or beholding, he realized, "I am a mess! Because I have unclean lips, and I live among people with unclean lips."

Isaiah saw that there is no comparison in the presence of the Lord. In seeing God as He is, we are all immediately confronted with our wretchedness, vileness, wickedness, and sinfulness, so much so that our only response is, *"Lord, I have sinned!"* We realize that we are not worthy of God's goodness and love. Ultimately, this is the only heart posture in which God can use us. We see that the angel uses hot coal to take away and purge iniquity and sin, and only after this is Isaiah approved to speak for God.

The irony in this passage is that God uses the same method for all who walk with Him. He asks us to keep our eyes on Him and not on one another. May God help us stop comparing ourselves with one another because that never leads us anywhere. Only when we compare ourselves with God and see ourselves for who we are can God begin our restoration process.

Everyday Good News Prayer

Heavenly Father, we thank you for this beautiful illustration revealed in the life of Isaiah for all of us to see. Free us from the deception of comparing ourselves with one another. May we behold You in all Your glory, majesty, and splendor and may that "beholding" change us forever. In Jesus's name, amen.

30

Jesus. Everyday Good News

THE ULTIMATE COMPARISON

Chernae Saka

My Reflections on "The Ultimate Comparison"

31

Jesus. Everyday Good News

SEEK FIRST

Chernae Saka

But seek ye first the kingdom of God, and his righteousness; and all these things shall be added unto you. (Matthew 6:33, KJV)

My mother's favorite scripture was Matthew 6:33, and now, being more mature, I understand why. In Matthew 6:25 and onward, Jesus lays the framework for us not to be anxious, saying, "*Take no thought.*" He emphasized not worrying about what to eat, drink, or wear. Naturally, our response might be perplexity because, according to Maslow's Hierarchy of Needs, the foundation of the pyramid includes physiological needs such as breathing, food, water, shelter, clothing, and sleep. These needs are the basic and bare minimum, and life cannot be sustained without them. However, Jesus tells us not to let these things be the first things we seek after. He instructs us to *"Seek ye first the kingdom of God and His righteousness."*

One might ask, *"What is the kingdom of God?"* According to Romans 14:17, the kingdom of God is righteousness, peace, and joy in the Holy Ghost. The kingdom of God is a different way of living life. Jesus said He is the way, the truth, and the life (John 14:6). The kingdom of God is a daily, conscious decision to surrender to Christ, follow Christ, and allow God's will to be done in your life. And, what about *"His"* righteousness? I emphasize *"His"* righteousness because, according to Isaiah 64:6, all *"our"* righteousness is as filthy rags. If we are to ever to stand in God's presence, we must have a perfect righteousness that exceeds that of the scribes and Pharisees (Matthew 5:20). Therefore, through God's love, mercy, and grace towards us, He gives us "*His*" righteousness, which is through faith in the actions of Jesus Christ (Romans 3:21-22). In other words, Jesus's death satisfies the Father's demands for perfect righteousness. Thus, we can only experience the benefits of "*His*" righteousness through faith in Christ's

SEEK FIRST

Chernae Saka

finished work on our behalf. We see an example of Matthew 6:33 lived out by King David and his son Solomon. King David, getting ready to retire, leaves his son parting words of wisdom. In 1 Chronicles 28:9, King David encourages Solomon to know God, serve Him with a perfect heart and a willing mind, and seek Him. Solomon heeds this advice after being anointed as the new King of Israel. He sacrifices to God first, and one night, God visits Solomon, asking what He can do for him. Solomon, instead of asking for wealth, honor, or long life, heeds his father's advice and asks for wisdom and knowledge on how to best govern God's people.

Solomon recognized his human limitations and great need for God's guidance. God granted him wisdom and knowledge, along with riches, wealth, and honor in response. No other king in Israel was treated as Solomon (1 Chronicles 1:1-13). Solomon became the wisest king in the land because he sought first the Kingdom of God and *"His"* righteousness.

Everyday Good News Prayer

Dear Heavenly Father, I thank You for this pointed reminder that I must seek You first in all that I do, not for the sake of gaining riches, wealth, and honor, but so that Your will is advanced in my life and the lives of my family. I know I that as I do so, You will care for me and provide for all my needs. I thank You, Lord. Amen.

31

Jesus. Everyday Good News

SEEK FIRST

Chernae Saka

My Reflections on "Seek First"

SECTION THREE

As broken people, we all need everyday good news about what Jesus has planned for us in the future.

32

Jesus. Everyday Good News

A BETTER COUNTRY AND CITY

Sharon Pergerson

But now they desire a better country, that is, an heavenly: wherefore God is not ashamed to be called their God: for he hath prepared for them a city. (Hebrews 11:16, KJV)

Hebrews chapter 11 is often called the faith chapter, and it is full of stories from those we would call examples of heroes of faith. In the chapter, faith is described as confident trust in the promises of God, even when the outcome is not in sight. Such faith is not passive; it drives action, obedience, and perseverance. Think about Abel, who offered a better sacrifice to God than his brother's, because his was based on His trust in God's promised Redeemer, who had not yet even come. Think about Noah, who was warned by God of things he could not see, such as a flood, when it had never even rained before. Noah trusted God's promise that there would be a flood, and so he built an ark as instructed, thus saving his family, with room for so many more.

Think about Abraham, who left his homeland, believing in the promise from God of a great inheritance he could not fully even grasp. Even when he got to the earthly land God gave him, He lived in a temporary tent because he was looking for a city with foundations which are built and made by God Himself. Think about Sarah, who finally, despite her old age and being past childbearing years, trusted that God would fulfill His promise to them and grant them a son through her. Why? because she judged God as One who faithfully keeps all His promises. All of these individuals and many more acted in faith, not knowing how or when God's promises would be fulfilled, yet they still believed all the way to the end of their lives.

The stories in Hebrews 11 also show that children of faith will go through challenges. Moses turned his back on Pharaoh's palace and

Jesus. Everyday Good News

A BETTER COUNTRY AND CITY

Sharon Pergerson

the opportunity to be king, to identify and suffer with God's people. Rahab risked her life to protect the spies. Others faced persecution, imprisonment, suffering, mistreatment, and death, yet they clung to the promises of God and looked forward to "a better country, a heavenly one" (Hebrews 11:16).

Today, followers of Jesus Christ still believe the same promises of God to return for all His children and take us to be with Him forever (John 14:1-3). We, too, are looking for a "better country, a heavenly one," one prepared for us by God Himself. We, too, have ups and downs, and things for us will probably appear to get worse before they get better. And, like our ancient brothers and sisters of faith, we too must keep our eyes on the prize and hold on to the promises of God no matter what, and despite the outcome not being in clear sight. We believe by faith that God will fulfill that promise to all of us from all ages together. Why? Because like Sarah, we have judged the Creator God, Jesus, as One who faithfully keeps all His promises.

Good News Prayer:

Lord, thank You for the Hebrews 11 examples of those who held on to your promises by faith. Strengthen my heart to continue to believe in your promises to me in good times and challenging times. Fill me with hope and courage as I run the race of faith set before me. Keep my eyes fixed on the prize of Your return for me, and on being with You forever. Thank you for being the Promise Keeper and for preparing a better country and city for all those put their trust in You. In Jesus' name, amen.

32

Jesus. Everyday Good News

A BETTER COUNTRY AND CITY

Sharon Pergerson

My Reflections on "A Better Country and City"

33

Jesus. Everyday Good News

NO MORE TEARS

Sharon Pergerson

"And God shall wipe away all tears from their eyes; and there shall be no more death, neither sorrow, nor crying, neither shall there be any more pain: for the former things are passed away. (Revelation 21:4, KJV)

Life can be overwhelming. For many, the weariness of daily struggles weighs heavily—whether it's physical exhaustion, emotional burnout, or simply feeling stretched too thin. Perhaps you're battling with cancer or caring for a loved one with cancer and suffering with them; it could be that every day you are reliving the pain of childhood abuse and trauma, navigating the aftermath of a broken relationship, weeping over your wandering child, or grieving the loss of someone dear. Or maybe you're just tired—tired of carrying burdens that feel too heavy to bear.

These experiences remind us that this world as it is now is not our forever home. As we read before, God has a special promise for all those who have chosen Jesus Christ as their Lord and Savior. One day, this life, with all its unbearable burdens, will end. In Revelation 21:4, after we are in Heaven, John saw Jesus wiping away all our tears, and there was no more death, sorrow, crying, or pain. In heaven, all of that will be over, forever. Picture Jesus, who knows every tear you've cried, every burden you've carried, and every pain you've suffered, wiping away your tears with His own nail-pierced hands and replacing them with His eternal love, health, peace, and joy.

What does that look like practically? For those who are enduring the painful journey of cancer or any terminal illness, Jesus has made heaven a place where our bodies are made new and free from disease. Notice, at the second coming, Jesus will change our sick bodies now subject to death to glorious bodies that can never die, like His body (1 Corinthians 15:51-57, Philippians 3:21).

33

Jesus. Everyday Good News

NO MORE TEARS

Sharon Pergerson

Thus, in heaven, there will be no more hospitals, dangerous medications and treatments, or goodbyes—only eternal life in perfect health, thank God. For those who have suffered abuse, trauma, or rejection, Jesus has made heaven a place of restoration and a life free from fear or harm. Even right now, He says to us, *"I will heal their waywardness and love them freely"* (Hosea 14:4, NIV). He tenderly replaces brokenness with His unfailing love and peace. *"The Lord is near to the brokenhearted and saves the crushed in spirit"* (Psalm 34:18, RSV).

For the grieving, Jesus promises heaven as a place that provides us the greatest hope: a reunion with fellow believers we love and have lost to death and eternal life with them in God's presence forever. (1 Thessalonians 4:16-17). Because of Jesus, death no longer has the final word; Jesus does. His sacrificial actions bought us eternal life beyond the grave, at His 2nd coming.

There is so much good news in Jesus. Thankfully, He doesn't wait until His great resurrection morning or until we get to heaven to ease our burdens, collect our tears, and bring us comfort. As has been repeated so many times before, He is with us right now. He is our present source of rest and help. Even now, when we are tired, remember Jesus sees us, He is with us, and He suffers with us. He promises us that when we come to Him with all our work, weariness, heavy burdens, and extreme pain and suffering, He will give us rest all the way to our soul level (Matt. 11:28). We all need that kind of rest every day.

In 2 Corinthians 4;16-17, and Romans 8:18, Paul encourages us not to lose heart or give up even though our physical bodies are wasting away, because even in this condition, God is continually renewing our spirit (our resolve to trust Him, our hope in Him and His promises). Paul also reminds us in Romans 8:18 that the struggles we face now, though real and painful, are light and only temporary (no matter how they feel) and they are working to produce God's glory (His character in us). Think about it, the truth that my struggles will result in producing the character of God in me, a weak, sinful human being, outweighs everything I could ever go through. In fact, my struggles are not even worth comparing to the glory God will reveal in me. Wow. May God help me, and you keep that ever in mind until He comes and delivers us and wipes away all the tears that come with death, sorrow, and pain.

Good News Prayer

Dear Father in Heaven, thank You for the promise of heaven, where You will wipe away our every tear and remove all pain, sorrow, and death. Strengthen me as I face life's overwhelming trials and struggles. Help me to fix my eyes on Jesus, my hope and joy. Help me to count the cost of my suffering with the eternal glory God is working in me. Keep comforting me and all others who are suffering right now and remind us of the eternal peace and joy awaiting us in Your presence, and in the heavenly home You are preparing for us. Thank You for Your mercy and kindness. In the name of Jesus, I pray, amen.

33

Jesus. Everyday Good News

NO MORE TEARS

Sharon Pergerson

My Reflections on "No More Tears"

34

Jesus. Everyday Good News

THE BRIDE IS COMING

Sharon Pergerson

" And he carried me away in the spirit to a great and high mountain, and shewed me that great city, the holy Jerusalem, descending out of heaven from God, having the glory of God: and her light was like unto a stone most precious, even like a jasper stone, clear as crystal." (Revelation 21:10-11, KJV)

Many people are scared to read the book of Revelation even though it is called the Revelation of Jesus Christ that God gave to let His children know what was coming in the future (Revelation 1:1). In fact, in verse 3, John pronounces a blessing on those who read it, listen to its prophecies, and hold on to those things written in it. We know by now that wherever Jesus is lifted up, there is good news for His children.

After the end of time and we have been in heaven for a while, John was shown a vision of the headquarters of God, the New Jerusalem, coming down from heaven like a bride beautifully dressed and ready for her groom (Revelation 21:2). Husbands, some of you remember the day your beautiful bride walked down the aisle coming to you and to publicly affirming her choice to be yours forever. You probably can't even fully describe how beautiful she looked to you. In Revelation chapters 18 to 21, John described the New Jerusalem city as a bride shining with the glory of God. Her walls were made of jasper, her foundations were adorned with every kind of precious stone, her twelve gates were made of single pearls, and her streets were made of pure, transparent gold. Can you imagine walking on streets of gold so radiant they gleam like crystal, and being surrounded by walls that glisten with jewels we can't even afford to touch right now?

In Revelation 21:22, John tells us he saw no temple in the city, no *place* to worship God why? Most likely because the entire city is the dwelling place of God the Father, Son, and Holy Spirit.

34

Jesus. Everyday Good News

THE BRIDE IS COMING

Sharon Pergerson

No longer will we need things or places to help us worship God. There, our focus will be solely on the Person due all our worship with no distractions or limitations, just pure, joyful praise and worship. Can you even imagine the living worship of God every day, in Person, all day, and having our minds "stayed" on Jesus all the time? Say amen with me if that sounds as good to you as it does to me.

In Revelation 21:23, John describes the city's source of light. He says there is no need for the sun or moon because the glory of God and the Lamb, Jesus, provides its light. Thus, there will be no more darkness, no shadows, and nothing to fear. The light of Christ will illuminate everything, bringing peace, joy, and clarity to all who dwell there. No wonder Jesus said in the beginning, *"Let there be light"* (Genesis 1:3); it came from Him. No wonder He told us in John 9:5 that He was the light of the World. He is the essence of light, and all in heaven will walk in His light. There, the gates will never be shut by day, for there is no night and nothing, and no one will ever enter with character traits that defy the character of God.

In Revelation 22:1-3, John was shown that flowing from the center of the New Jerusalem was the river of the water of life, clear as crystal, coming from the throne of God and the Lamb. On either side of the river stood the tree of life, bearing fruit every month and leaves for the healing of the nations. Of course, there will be no more brokenness, sickness, or strife there. God's healing will be complete, and life will flourish eternally. I believe partaking of the healing leaves, which are watered by the river of life that flows from the throne of God and the lamb, are for sustaining our perpetual health and well-being. Praise God, I am looking forward to that.

34

Jesus. Everyday Good News

THE BRIDE IS COMING

Sharon Pergerson

For me, the greatest aspect of the New Jerusalem is that God Himself will dwell with us, His people, fulfilling His promise to be with us forever. John shared that he "*heard a loud voice from the throne saying, 'Look! God's dwelling place is now among the people, and He will dwell with them. They will be His people, and God Himself will be with them and be their God" (Revelation 21:3, KJV).* No longer will there be separation, sin, or anything that hinders our relationship with God. We will live in perpetual, perfect communion with Him.

The New Jerusalem city may seem like only a future hope; however, in Christ, it is a reality as sure as His existence. So, no matter what challenges we face today, remember that Jesus Christ has prepared a home for you—a place of unimaginable beauty, peace, and joy. Paul encourages us in 2 Corinthians 5:1, *"For we know that if the earthly tent we live in is destroyed, we have a building from God, an eternal house in heaven, not built by human hands" (KJV).* Thus, whenever life feels overwhelming, let's keep fixing our eyes on Jesus and what He has in store for us, and it will fill us with hope, strength, and peace; He is our surety that one day soon, we will walk those golden streets and live forever in His presence.

Good News Prayer

Dear Father in Heaven, thank You for the promise of the New Jerusalem—a place of perfect beauty and peace where I will dwell with You forever. Help me to hold on to this hope when life feels heavy. Strengthen my faith and remind me daily that You are preparing a place for me that is beyond anything I can imagine. Thank You for Your eternal love and for making a way for me to live forever. In Jesus's name I pray, amen.

34

Jesus. Everyday Good News

THE BRIDE IS COMING

Sharon Pergerson

My Reflections on "The Bride is Coming"

35

Jesus. Everyday Good News

BACK TO THE BOSOM

Sharon Pergerson

Father, I will that they also, whom thou hast given Me, be with Me where I am; that they may behold My glory, which thou hast given Me: for thou lovedst Me before the foundation of the world. (John 17:24, KJV)

I have always been fascinated with what Heaven and the new earth will be like. I imagine I will break down on the ground in tears, realizing I made it. I imagine myself almost fainting when Jesus holds me in His arms. I imagine looking into the eyes of my formerly deceased loved ones, and there is only silence and salty tears pouring down our faces. I can also imagine walking among the beauty and wealth of heaven with a trembling voice, thanking God that He got me here and gave me this beyond-magnificent place to be my very own forever home. Just being there is more than I could have ever wished for.

Then, while studying, I saw something beautiful in the Bible that dulled my sweet imagination. In John 1:18, John shared something about Jesus that floored me and led me to write this thought. *"No man hath seen God at any time, the only begotten Son, which is in the bosom of the Father, He hath declared Him" (KJV).* In reading this text, I noticed where Jesus was, "in the bosom of the Father." That word is not in all versions of the Bible. However, it conveys the thought that Jesus was in the closest and unbroken fellowship with the Father, where He had the most perfect knowledge of the Father and the closest intimate friendship and mutual love with Him. In the bosom is the closest relationship possible in the universe, one so tightly knit that nothing or no one can break it, and one that is in perpetual harmonious unity.

That's the "state" of the relationship between God the Father, God the Son, and God the Holy Spirit. Zech. 13:7 makes a similar point. *"Awake, O sword, against My Shepherd, and against the Man that is My fellow, saith the Lord of hosts..."*

35

Jesus. Everyday Good News

BACK TO THE BOSOM

Sharon Pergerson

Here God is expressing His pain in having to smite Jesus, who is His Fellow (the One near and dear to Him, One of the same Divine nature, His co-equal Person in glory and majesty, His Companion, His Associate, One who has a perfect knowledge of Him, and is closest to His heart, thought, and affections). Nothing we have seen or experienced on earth compares to such a relationship (though marriage, despite sin, was designed to give us a tiny, tiny, microscopic snippet of it).

My writing is faulty, but I am praying that you can grasp, as best as we sinful human beings can, the oneness, friendship, and intimacy of the relationship between the Father, Son, and Holy Spirit, for they are one. In John 16:27-28, Jesus reiterates that closeness, "*For the Father himself loveth you, because ye have loved Me, and have believed that I came out from God. I came forth from the Father, and am come into the world: again, I leave the world, and go to the Father" (KJV).* Jesus means for us to understand a glimpse of it and believe it for a reason.

In His prayer to God His Father, right before His arrest, Jesus kept asking that His children be one, as They are One, and that they be with Him where He is (John 17:5, 8, 13, 20-26). In John 14:1-3, Jesus promised to come again and receive us to Himself so that where He is, we may be also. I believe Jesus was talking about so much more than taking us to a place with mansions, streets of gold, and where life will be forever. Jesus was also talking about getting you and me to where He abides, in the bosom of the Father. Jesus wants us to be a part of their close relationship. I believe His prayer in John 17 was about asking that we be allowed to join their relationship, fellowship, oneness, and bosom inner circle. He was praying that we get to experience being a part of the close relationship He has with His Father.

35

Jesus. Everyday Good News

BACK TO THE BOSOM

Sharon Pergerson

He is praying that one day, our hearts and minds will be joined with theirs, and we will become part of the closest fellowship in existence, one that is so tight and strong that nothing and no one can break it; one that is in perpetual, harmonious unity.

If we think about it, the intent of Satan and sin was to eternally rip apart all that was meant to be close to God. However, in Jesus Christ, God risked everything to save us and get us into the place Jesus willed and prayed that we be. Jesus's heartfelt prayer was that we, who are so foul, so selfish, so cruel, and so helpless, the very ones who pierced Him in His bosom and caused Him indescribable grief and agony, be welcomed into God's intimate family circle. What a God, what a God! Who in their right mind can resist and reject such love? Not me.

Jesus did all that He did not just to return and take us to a magnificent place, but also to restore you and me to the relationship He created us to be a part of, the closest, strongest relationship in the universe, to be with Him in the bosom of the Father. The good news for us today and every day is that this sweet fellowship Jesus willed for us and prayed to the Father for can begin in our lives today, right now. God is not angry with you nor me; He wants this closeness even more than we do, so much so that He paid the ultimate price to guarantee it happens. Read 2 Corinthians 5:18-20 (RSV):

> *"All this is from God, who through Christ reconciled us to himself and gave us the ministry of reconciliation; that is, in Christ God was reconciling the world to himself, not counting their trespasses against them, and entrusting to us the message of reconciliation. So we are ambassadors for Christ, God making his appeal through us. We beseech you, on behalf of Christ, to be reconciled to God."*

35

Jesus. Everyday Good News

BACK TO THE BOSOM

Sharon Pergerson

In Christ, God brought us reconciliation. He changed the status of our alienated relationship with Him and set us on the path of closeness, intimacy, fellowship, and oneness that will never end and will culminate in heaven, in His presence, for the ceaseless ages of eternity. Wow. The only call left is your response: will you choose to be reconciled to Him? Will you positively respond to all that God has done for you in Jesus Christ? If so, Jesus is and always will be your everyday good news, and eternal life begins today for you.

As you ponder all that you have read in these 35 devotional *thoughts*, read or sing the words of this song by musician Andrae Crouch:

"How can I say thanks for the things you have done for me?
Things so undeserved yet You gave to prove Your love for me.
The voices of a million angels could not express my gratitude.
All that I am and ever hope to be I owe it all to Thee. To God be the glory, to God be the glory, to God be the glory For the things He has done..."

Good News Prayer:

Dear Jesus, thank you for coming to me from the bosom of the Father. Thank You for leaving the safest, sweetest, most loving relationship in the universe to live with sinful humans like me. What wondrous love that You prayed to the Father that I get to be a part of Your bosom relationship, and You gave your life to ensure it. All I can say is thank You and receive You into my heart, today and every day.

35

Jesus. Everyday Good News

BACK TO THE BOSOM

Sharon Pergerson

My Reflections on "Back to the Bosom"

About the Authors

Sharon M. Pergerson is a published author and educator. She has taught multiple ages and develops faith-based educational curricula, workshops, retreats, programs, and courses. Her greatest passion is basking in the beauty and power of Christ's character and helping others see its benefits for themselves. She believes that when Christ is lifted up, His loving character draws people to Him. Sharon especially loves to share how knowing Christ in dark, painful times provides the power for healing, stability, and resilience. Sharon is a lifelong learner, leader, and innovator. Sharon holds a Ph.D. in Organizational Leadership which helped to better equip her to lead and nurturing up-and-coming leaders. Sharon and her family love people and have spent their lives in service to others in different parts of the world. She enjoys writing, traveling, sewing, and cooking. Sharon and her two adult children, William III and Jaissa, live in Houston, TX.

Chernae Saka is a wife, mother, teacher, and, most importantly, a child of God. Though she grew up in church, she can now see, in hindsight, how God has been faithfully ordering her steps throughout life and drawing her into deeper intimacy with Him. Chernae is passionate about sharing "The Everlasting Gospel of Jesus Christ" and its transformative power in people's lives. When she is not writing, Chernae finds joy in exhorting and encouraging others along life's journey. She also cherishes spending time with her family and exploring God's great outdoors, both of which remind her of God's boundless Agape love for all. Her hope is that the "thoughts' in this book will inspire readers to take God seriously, seek His face in all things, and trust in His Word. Her prayer is that each thought will bring comfort to readers, guide them to the One who loves them most, and leave them clearly seeing how blessed and beloved they are! Chernae and her husband Emmanuel live in Nashville, TN, with their two sons, Jahaziel and Eliel.

Oliver Edward Nelson III is a civil rights lawyer by trade, but his first love is the sharing the everlasting gospel, specifically with those who have never been exposed to the marvelous truth of God's love for them in Christ. He and his beautiful wife Charity share this love and believe that sharing and more importantly living this gospel message is what will hasten the coming of our Lord and Savior Jesus Christ. Oliver and Charity live in Minneapolis, MN, have been married for twenty-three years, and have two adult children, Oliver IV and Jasmine.

Made in the USA
Columbia, SC
29 May 2025

58636048R00074